Unleash the immense potential of strategically utilising Super Users to drive lasting advantages for your implementation projects and ensure your organisation's longevity. This book serves as a practical guide, tailored for pragmatic individuals, providing invaluable insights for practitioners in systems implementations, change management, and organisational projects. Its research-based foundation is seamlessly blended with real-world applications, making it an indispensable companion for anyone seeking hands-on expertise in driving successful transformations.

Colin German FBCS,
Co-Founder and Senior Consultant, CMG Consulta

This book is well-written and provides a wealth of knowledge, advice, and real-world examples, on successful and collaborative Super User communities. The author's use of humour made the book an enjoyable and engaging read, it will be a resource I refer to again. I highly recommend this book to anyone involved in digital transformation or software projects.

Mike Button CITP MBCS,
ICT Infrastructure and Development Manager

This book presents the case for Super Users and their active participation in the system development life-cycle with rigour and clarity. It is a thorough piece that provides both underpinning theory and practical steps to facilitate successful project outcomes through the identification, development and inclusion of Super Users. There is a wealth of practical advice on how Super Users can positively and productively interact with the wide variety of possible stakeholders in the project lifecycle.

John Burns LLM CEng MBCS,
Information Security Risk Analyst

An excellent guide for creating, developing and maintaining Super User Networks in any high complexity or high impact digital transformation or software project. It also importantly covers when not to use them, and the considerations, potential pitfalls and mitigation strategies. Grounded in both practice and research, the book helpfully signposts to change management models, frameworks and methodologies. Explains how Super Users can be effectively deployed as part of a multi-faceted change and continuous improvement process.

Barry McGuire MBCS,
Systems Librarian

This is not the usual business book, it approaches the topic with a sense of humour, the author's personality shines through backed by a wealth of experience and expertise. Highlighting the power of leveraging Super Users in your software project with step-by-step how to implement a Super User model from initiation through to Business as Usual. It holds insightful key takeaways on top of well thought out methods for adoption.

Kym Glover MBCS,
Program Manager, ForgeRock

Embracing champions, super users and agents of change in digital transformation is a marker of successful people centred change. *Super User Networks for Software Projects* provides tips to navigate recognised change management models combined with a psychological depth that gives confidence to any change practitioner, project manager or transformation leader.

Jim Bird CMgr MCMI,
Management Consultant

SUPER USER NETWORKS FOR SOFTWARE PROJECTS

BCS, THE CHARTERED INSTITUTE FOR IT

BCS, The Chartered Institute for IT, is committed to making IT good for society. We use the power of our network to bring about positive, tangible change. We champion the global IT profession and the interests of individuals, engaged in that profession, for the benefit of all.

Exchanging IT expertise and knowledge
The Institute fosters links between experts from industry, academia and business to promote new thinking, education and knowledge sharing.

Supporting practitioners
Through continuing professional development and a series of respected IT qualifications, the Institute seeks to promote professional practice tuned to the demands of business. It provides practical support and information services to its members and volunteer communities around the world.

Setting standards and frameworks
The Institute collaborates with government, industry and relevant bodies to establish good working practices, codes of conduct, skills frameworks and common standards. It also offers a range of consultancy services to employers to help them adopt best practice.

Become a member
Over 70,000 people including students, teachers, professionals and practitioners enjoy the benefits of BCS membership. These include access to an international community, invitations to a roster of local and national events, career development tools and a quarterly thought-leadership magazine. Visit www.bcs.org/membership to find out more.

Further information
BCS, The Chartered Institute for IT,
3 Newbridge Square,
Swindon, SN1 1BY, United Kingdom.
T +44 (0) 1793 417 417
(Monday to Friday, 09:00 to 17:00 UK time)
www.bcs.org/contact
http://shop.bcs.org/

SUPER USER NETWORKS FOR SOFTWARE PROJECTS
Best practices for training and change management

By Jayne Mather

Published by BCS Learning and Development Ltd, a wholly owned subsidiary of BCS, The Chartered Institute for IT, 3 Newbridge Square, Swindon, SN1 1BY, UK.
www.bcs.org

Paperback ISBN: 978-1-78017-6109
PDF ISBN: 978-1-78017-6116
ePUB ISBN: 978-1-78017-6123

British Cataloguing in Publication Data.
A CIP catalogue record for this book is available at the British Library.

Disclaimer:
The views expressed in this book are of the authors and do not necessarily reflect the views of the Institute or BCS Learning and Development Ltd except where explicitly stated as such. Although every care has been taken by the authors and BCS Learning and Development Ltd in the preparation of the publication, no warranty is given by the authors or BCS Learning and Development Ltd as publisher as to the accuracy or completeness of the information contained within it and neither the authors nor BCS Learning and Development Ltd shall be responsible or liable for any loss or damage whatsoever arising by virtue of such information or any instructions or advice contained within this publication or by any of the aforementioned.

All URLs were correct at the time of publication.

Publisher's acknowledgements
Reviewers: Colin German, David Hannell
Publisher: Ian Borthwick
Sales director: Charles Rumball
Commissioning editor: Heather Wood
Production manager: Florence Leroy
Project manager: Sunrise Setting Ltd
Copy-editor: Gillian Bourn
Proofreader: Barbara Eastman
Indexer: David Gaskell
Cover design: Alex Wright
Cover image: Shutterstock/dima_zel
Typeset by Lapiz Digital Services, Chennai, India

CONTENTS

LIST OF FIGURES AND TABLES

AUTHOR

Jayne Mather is an experienced IT professional with over 25 years of experience initiating and working on projects to implement software and technology into global organisations. She has led on testing, training, change management and business process on 14 successful software projects, at the last count, as well as extensive work on technology curriculum development and software training content.

Throughout her career she has seen what works and actively embraced new methods and techniques, adding them to her toolkit. With a passion for IT systems and emerging technology, Jayne is determined to spread her enthusiasm to end users, leading to more successful technology adoption and return on investment for organisations.

Jayne's academic credentials include an MBA, and CIPD in Learning & Development. She is a certified developer and instructor for Blue Prism® Intelligent Automation and a certified Architect for the Blue Prism® Robotic Operating Model™. These credentials enable her to combine theory with experience to create a compelling case for why Super Users are an invaluable asset to deploy on any digital transformation project.

FOREWORD

Jayne Mather knows the magic.

With years of practical experience and leadership, Jayne lays out her insights and advice for all hoping to unlock the magic of the super user.

Super users are the key to a successful implementation of any software system. Their technical insight is important to the design and evolution for the system, but their critical role is as a respected key opinion leader. They are often the go-to person in their department and the trust they engender gives the users the confidence they need to engage with and embrace the new system and processes.

Moreover, the social impact of super users cannot be overstated, as they create an environment of success and foster momentum. Acting as conduits into their departments, they serve as the eyes and ears of the project team, offering assistance in testing, troubleshooting, and preparing their colleagues for the transition. Super users know how the department functions today, how it will succeed tomorrow, and the critical metrics that will need to be monitored to ensure everything is on track. They know the business and they know the people at a practical hands-on level.

Go live is when the magic happens. This is the moment that makes all the investment in super users worthwhile. Back in their role, super users can lead, train, problem solve and, most importantly, triage the issues on behalf of the customers and the business. No one can gainsay them. It is a leadership position without parallel and delivers outstanding personal growth potential.

To all you program leaders, this is the moment to become the servant leader. Listen to your super users and clear their path to a successful go live. Pass the baton to them at go live and cheer them on!

Good luck in finding and nurturing your super users. They know the answers and will deliver the successful change.

I hope I've convinced you to read on and of the magic to come!

Dr. Tony Hopwood, Transformation Director

ACKNOWLEDGEMENTS

For my son Ethan James, who is proud of me and writes me notes telling me to never give up. Right back at you kid, you'll achieve amazing things and the world is brighter now you're in it.

Thanks to my small, but very high quality, circle of my partner, family and friends. You love my geeky side as much as my party side, and have always let me be my true self around you. Adrian, who gave me love and support and spent hours with me listening to my ideas and reading the book. Mum, dad and Stuart – you always did say I should be a writer, thank you. Rachel, Hazel, Lisa, Stacey, Caroline and Michelle – thanks for the love and the belief and the laughs. And for the knowledge that I am apparently the Chandler of the group as no one actually knows, or maybe cares, what it is that I do for a living – hopefully this now helps explain it.

To the leaders and project professionals I have worked with in my career. You've showed why mentoring not managing is the key to growth in your people. I hope you can see everything I have learned from you in these pages.

Thanks to Heather and Ian at BCS who believed in the book, and to the talented reviewers who saw the value it could bring to organisations; I'm very grateful for your insights and contributions.

Thanks to you, the reader; not only do I hope you enjoyed the book, but I hope you can continue to evangelise within your own institutions that Super Users are for life, not just for Go Live.

Please do connect with me on LinkedIn, and I would be excited to hear your thoughts and ideas on how we can continue to promote Super User networks as best practice methodology for training and change management in software projects.

www.linkedin.com/in/jayne-mather/

WHO IS THIS BOOK FOR?

If you work in any of the following roles or have an interest in any of the following areas, this book is for you:

- Software Super User
- Training
- HR or talent management
- Change management
- Project management
- Software expert
- Change agent
- Digital transformation leader
- Continuous improvement
- Product managers or owners
- Super User leader
- Learning and development or education services
- IT
- Internal communications
- Agile leader
- Organisational design
- Technology evangelist
- Community leader
- Senior leaders and executives
- Software implementation

By the end of this book you will be able to:

- Educate organisations on how to initiate and maintain a Super User network.
- Utilise approaches to realise the benefits of employing Super Users throughout all software project phases.
- Provide the impetus needed to sustain the Super User network for the whole software life cycle to enhance product adoption and make a return on investment.
- Offer best practice methodology that adopts technology solutions for the long term.

HOW TO USE THIS BOOK

When I read a business book, I go to the contents page and to the index and I pick out the parts I need and just go to those sections. But I promise you, this isn't your average business book.

This book has been written to give you an entertaining read from cover to cover; it uses my personality, enthusiasm and humour to educate and compel you to use these best practice techniques for the training and change management activities needed in your software projects. Software projects aren't boring; this book will prove that. We'll enjoy ourselves through each project phase and each chapter.

But it also contains plenty to back it up from my years of experience and breadth of study. You'll find theories, models, diagrams, case studies and practical advice that will enable you to put this book to good use, as well as some new frameworks written especially for this edition.

Part I of the book establishes the basics for the training and change management methodology for your project – why you need Super Users, the value they bring throughout the project phases and some of the tasks you should be getting them involved in. Particularly check out Chapter 3 to give you a visual sequence of the steps covered in this book.

Part II will give you a practical, deeper dive into those tasks so you can apply the steps of creating and sustaining a Super User network into your software project.

Part III is where it gets interesting, with the theories, models, research and evidence for why this methodology works.

Part IV makes the final case on how you can use a Super User network to make your software project a success. Don't miss the final chapter, which includes key takeaways and advice from digital transformation leaders.

You really shouldn't miss a single part or chapter. If you're not sure of anything, check out the glossary and if your interest is piqued head to the further reading section to add to your reading list; there's also some really interesting sources in the references section to give you a deeper dive into some of the concepts. Only after all that should you head to the index; there you'll find where each of our key terms are mentioned, and you can head back to those pages to read them again.

Read on and learn how to make your software projects a super success.

PART I
YOUR INTRODUCTION TO SUPER USER NETWORKS
'The Why'

- Build a compelling proposal to outline the benefits of implementing a Super User network and articulate how it can improve the success of your software project and organisational culture.

- Determine if a Super User is the right role for your software project in accordance with your project aims and role requirements.

- Design a comprehensive plan for creating and utilising a Super User network throughout all phases of your software project.

- Define the specific responsibilities of Super Users during each phase of the software project, including tasks such as testing, training and troubleshooting.

1   WHY DO WE NEED SUPER USERS?

Creating the business case for a Super User network to deliver training and change management for your software project.

Digital transformation is imperative to ensure your business remains competitive and efficient. Strategically integrating digital technologies and solutions to sustain, modernise, improve and optimise your organisation can mean big transformational projects. This book will help you to implement those projects successfully using best practice recommendations in training and change management specifically for introducing new software.

When rolling out a new system or technology to your organisation, a proven technique is using a network of Super Users.

> A Super User is an expert in both software and business processes, and provides the link between your software end users and your project team.

Why do we need this role?

It is going to depend on a lot of factors: how complex the system is that you are rolling out, how many unique departments or functions you have, how big is the change, how many end users are affected and the extent of the training resource that you need. If the answers to any of these questions imply the change impact is low, the complexity is low and the number of end users is low – then you do not need Super Users; your training team can and should be the only resource you need. Rarely though does a new system implementation or a technology project fall into these categories, so we need Super Users to help us transition during the project work, the rollout and beyond.

Super Users can make a real difference to the adoption and success of your project, from the design stage to end user support. Throughout this book we will explore all the best practice recommendations concerned with utilising Super Users to the maximum benefit, but let us first explore further why we need them.

INFLUENCE END USERS

Your Super User's primary purpose is to be a positive influence on your end users: to get them using the right transactions, the right ways of working and exhibiting the desired behaviours. Your Super Users will not only support them but will be the role model for them to emulate.

Not everyone is a huge geek like me and loves IT systems, but you want your Super Users to love your systems and for that enthusiasm to spread to your end users. You want your end users to eventually feel that it is easy to follow the right process and it should make their roles easier to perform – if you have built the system right, of course, but that is a whole different book right there.

GET BUY-IN

We will discuss change management a little later and the crucial role your Super Users will play, but you need Super Users to help you gain buy-in to the change. The Super Users will help you to communicate why the change is necessary, so users can look forward to the change and the benefits it will bring to them. They will help you to answer and pre-empt questions, convey the future vision and eliminate frustration caused by learning the new processes.

LOCAL EXPERTISE

You should aim to leave expertise within each local team; you do not want the knowledge and advanced understanding of a system to sit only in the brains of your project or training team. Otherwise, what happens when they move on to other projects, systems or even other organisations? We need Super Users so that when a new system becomes business as usual, the expertise remains in place in each department. This will help to maintain end user confidence and adherence to processes from having continuing support from the Super User.

CROSS-FUNCTIONAL COLLABORATION

Every modern business knows they need to increase cross-functional working across departments to become more dynamic at getting things done. Super Users are a fantastic way to achieve this. Each department or team may still operate in their own bubble, but by using a community of Super Users who regularly speak and network, you get them operating outside their silos. You get them to work together to improve processes, communicate and solve frustrations between teams, share ways of working and above all increase the efficiency of flow between each function. This is why supporting and facilitating this group of Super Users to become a community is so important to success and will be addressed in its own chapter.

CONTINUAL END USER TRAINING

End users never need training only once: you will have new staff, your new system will have enhancements or upgrades, there will be changes to ways of working, new processes, or there may be performance improvement initiatives. Super Users should remain involved and be responsible for training in whatever capacity you decide: group or one to one or supplying training materials. If you do not have Super Users, then what is the alternative? A continual demand on your training team for refresher training or new colleagues receiving a different level of training depending on who they sit next to.

Super Users are not just for Go Live, they are for life. (You will hear this catchphrase a lot from me.) Ensure this concept is captured in your Super User role profile and that management are committed to this fact. Super Users can then continue to be the nominated trainer for their group, can continue to add or improve training material and should be the go-to person for onboarding new colleagues. This ensures consistency and maintains the high standards that your Super Users champion.

DEPLOYMENT DURING ROLLOUT

Super Users should be used to deliver training to your end users in advance of Go Live, as well as cascading information and comms messages. Use them throughout your implementation schedule, deploying them in key locations as your training resource. Super Users will be trained by your training team or your project team. But end users will receive training from people they are likely to know and trust. It removes the demand for a small training team to be at each site and should therefore reduce the time it takes to roll out your new system, as these training activities can take place simultaneously, rather than a staged calendar of events provided by one resource.

SUPPORT SERVICE

I am fairly sure you will have an IT helpdesk, but they should be dealing with issues where something is not working. IT should not be dealing with 'How Do I' questions, so we need Super Users to solicit and respond to those questions from the teams they are looking after. This enables a portfolio of frequently asked questions to be built up and allows the answers to be shared among all Super Users and to build knowledge in all teams. We should capture and measure these 'How Do I' queries in the beginning to share results and seek advice from the full Super User community. This empowers your Super Users to be problem solvers in your organisation and frees up your IT resource for their primary purpose.

MAINTAIN BEST PRACTICE

Your Super Users champion the best ways of working and they should be capable of addressing poor performance in their teams, either through offering training or pointing out trends to an escalation point. If you are not using Super Users for training, then bad habits can spread: that 'bodge' people do to get past an error message will become the norm, and knowledge will begin to dilute over time. We will be continually ensuring that Super Users receive training to maintain advanced knowledge, and they will then in turn do the same for the end users, passing on tips, easy ways of working, troubleshooting techniques and, above all, the correct ways of doing things.

RETAIN KNOWLEDGE

Have you ever been in an office where there are sticky notes over every person's screen with things to remember or notebooks full of scribbled instructions that they need to complete a process? These are advertisements to you that training support is needed. Super Users should feed these requirements back into your training team, help to create or suggest training material and ensure all your end users have the knowledge they need to do their job. They will provide training or materials (we will cover the options for materials in another chapter) and ensure the knowledge is retained in your users without the need for all those messy sticky notes. OK, pet hate, you've caught me.

Retaining knowledge may also be provided by way of coaching support or further training sessions, which may not have been planned in your implementation schedule. It is rare that end users will attend one training session and remember everything they need; with Super Users in place you fill this gap with that local expertise and support service to ensure those learning at a different pace can continue to develop their aptitude on your software.

TALENT DEVELOPMENT

You already have people in your organisation who love to help others; those people in your department who are the go-to person or the 'fount of all knowledge'. Identifying and utilising these people as Super Users harnesses, rewards and empowers those strengths for the good of everyone. It is my experience that Super Users often see career progression after they have been given the opportunity to show their strengths in a formal capacity. This is absolutely something to be desired, that those with business process expertise, people skills and technical know-how can be developed for future assignments or even, just as desired, to enhance the performance of their existing team. This is why we explore in another chapter, about recruiting Super Users, that we want the 'best of the best' to begin with.

RETAIN STAFF

Retaining skilled and experienced staff is essential to maintain organisational continuity, promote growth and achieve strategic objectives. When end users are trained well and equipped with the appropriate tools, they are more likely to feel competent and confident in their roles, which can enhance their job satisfaction and commitment. Ensuring your end users have the capability, and the right tools and training to do their jobs can have an impact on their willingness to stay in the role, can reduce turnover costs and secure stability in the workforce.

INCREASE END USER KNOWLEDGE

You will have heard the phrase 'people don't know what they don't know', which is very true with systems. If they've only had training on a few screens to begin with, then they may not know that there is another screen with a report in it that will be beneficial to them, replacing hours of manual work in spreadsheets. By continuing to provide training and sharing knowledge among our Super User community we can ensure that reports, variants, queries, troubleshooting, shortcuts and more are passed on to our end users – continually adding to the knowledge that they had at Go Live.

ENHANCE BUSINESS PROCESS UNDERSTANDING

Your staff are not there just to push buttons in the order that they were told to; they need to understand that they are fulfilling a requirement and executing a business process. They need to know why they are pushing those buttons in that order. Super Users will have that knowledge passed to them, which they will spread to end users through demonstrating, explaining and answering questions. It will help people to understand the flow of work between departments, the implications of each button press and what they are achieving each time they press save or run.

Super Users can be your voice as to why you have invested in a new system, why you're changing ways of working and why a business process is executed as it is. Give them the tools to articulate this to their colleagues in a compelling manner. As the renowned author and speaker Simon Sinek says, 'Start with The Why'.[1] We love that one in the training space.

COST OF ERRORS

Have you ever done an exercise to look at inaccuracy, the cost of complaints or resolving errors? I recommend you do, and that you use your Super Users to address this. Super Users can be used to highlight these trends or errors, to offer solutions or training to prevent them and to educate end users in the cause and effect of inaccuracies. Do not just use your Super Users for training: get them involved in your preventive cause analysis exercises; get them suggesting ways of working process improvements; and use their expertise to your advantage. Can you see yet why it is so important to keep Super Users in that role after Go Live? Keeping that community going can pay huge dividends in ensuring productivity continually improves, by having that resource and expertise always in place.

WHEN NOT TO USE SUPER USERS

As we have already discussed, if a system rollout is low complexity, low change impact or a small number of users then Super Users should not be necessary. But I would recommend you rethink using Super Users if you are not going to commit to using this community **after** Go Live. What if performance dips, or what if there is another project or a new enhancement or a new way of working; are you just going to start again to recruit new Super Users or put the demand back onto your training team? How will new colleagues be trained if there are no software experts in-house? If you are not keeping them, do not use them.

You need to commit to keeping your Super User community alive long after Go Live. Who will own this, who will bring the community together, who will collate training needs and lessons learned from them? I am more than happy to say it again and again that Super Users are for life and not just the life of your project. If you can only commit to

---

1   Sinek, S. (2009) *How great leaders inspire action*, TED. https://www.ted.com/talks/simon_sinek_how_great_leaders_inspire_action

supporting these users for the length of your project, perhaps a change agent may be more suitable for you. We will discuss the difference in the next chapter, but a Super User remains a Super User, long after everyone has forgotten the project name.

It is important you ensure senior and middle managers are bought into the Super User concept from the beginning; you need them to be supported by their managers in using a portion of their time and role to support and train end users. Send those guys to me. I will happily talk all day about the downfalls of not having Super Users and the benefits management will reap from supporting your wonderfully super Super Users. Have I convinced you yet as to why you need Super Users? More to come...

Creating a business case for a Super User network:

☑ Engage with the project sponsor

☑ Recruit allies who have experience with Super User networks

☑ Articulate the benefits mentioned in this chapter

☑ Align the benefits to the project vision and business goals

☑ Describe the risks of not using Super Users

2 IS A SUPER USER THE RIGHT ROLE FOR YOUR SOFTWARE PROJECT?

The key differences between the roles of Super User, change agent, key user and more, to enable you to determine which role is the best fit for your software project.

This book focuses on Super Users, but the techniques discussed here can be applied to key users, change agents and subject matter experts. So, are they all the same thing by a different name? Not necessarily, and you need to choose the right one for your organisation and choose the name of the role that fits best.

Let us have a look at some definitions.

Super User

The Super User is a business process expert who will also become a system expert. They are the link between your project or software team and the end users of your system. Crucial here is that the Super User is a role that lasts for as long as your system lasts.

A simple explanation for a Super User is 'Someone who is an expert in the software and can help other people to use it.'

Change agent

This group of people are tasked with embedding the change into the organisation, using recognised change management techniques. They have influence over your stakeholders and end users, and they focus on helping your people manage the impact of change. They may coincidentally be system experts, they may be process experts, but these are not necessary to this role – they are here to help your organisation transform. The difference here is that a change agent remains for the life of the project; once the change is considered to be part of 'business as usual' the role is complete. If you are implementing a system, you need Super Users to stay with the system to continue the training, best practice and enhancement activities. Super Users are, and should be, business as usual.

Subject matter expert (SME)

An SME is the resident authority on a particular topic; they have the relevant knowledge and expertise to pass on to others. We may use an SME to educate key people in the project, to consult on business decisions and to help the business understand the implications of changes, consult on training content or on regulatory or compliance implications. The SME will always be that expert but are likely to have their own role to perform; they are there to be the knowledge expert for your leadership and project teams, not to influence your end users. An SME is a suitable choice for a Super User but still the Super User role is different and is expected to be involved in more activities than the SME.

Key user

A key user on a software project is a key resource for training and embedding your solution. They have specific duties at cutover and in training provision, but they are an additional resource to support your Super Users and have been given a small head start on your end users. In all honesty, in my experience, if you have had to bring in key users, then you did not have enough Super Users to begin with. If you've had to bring in key users to help you provide training for the solution, and help your end users, and you've already given them advanced training – for the purpose of sustaining the Super User community, I recommend you welcome them into the fold here and retain that resource.

Power user

Often referred to in Microsoft systems, a power user may also be someone with systems knowledge but is typically someone who has more systems access than other users. Perhaps they have administration permissions for user management, configuration changes, master data amendments or other access you may want to restrict from general use. Occasionally this extra access may benefit a Super User, but Super Users do so much more than this.

Citizen developer

You can use similar methods described in this book if you have citizen developers, but again they are a different concept to Super Users as they need to receive training, not deliver it, but they do need a dedicated training programme that you can use this book to formulate. I would describe these as advanced users of software based within the business, not IT, and outside a core development team. Typically using no-code or low-code applications such as automation or business intelligence tools, they can enhance the adoption of new technology and maximise the benefits by accelerating the rollout among their business areas. A citizen developer would need advanced system training – but this could be training delivered by Super Users, or mentors in your core team, someone with expert knowledge who can guide them in the technical skills as well as best practice standards and governance.

WHICH ROLE IS BEST FOR MY PROJECT?

A Super User becomes a hybrid of a change agent, SME and system specialist. They are trained to support users of the system or processes, cascade comms, enact continuous improvement and be responsible for change management, and they stay in this role. We develop them to become an essential role for your organisation; if you use them right, they will always be needed in this role. You have invested thousands if not millions in your chosen software; use your Super Users to help you make the most of this investment and focus on making sure your end users use it for the desired benefits, now and in the future.

Change agents can be brilliant roles, but you need to ensure you are selecting what you really need. What does the life cycle of your chosen software look like? How many teams and processes does it touch? How complex is your system? What is the focus for you? Is it using the system or is it embedding an organisational change? For example, an online holiday system may be a substantial change for a business that is used to verbal or paper requests, but it might be a low complexity, off-the-shelf system. This may be considered a big culture change that you need change agents to help with. But will you need Super Users to continue to work with the system developers and to continue to test, train and deliver improvements for the system? Or once the system and change is in, is it then business as usual? This example may be more suitable to a change agent, as the key differentiator is a change agent stays with the project while a Super User stays with the system.

A change agent can be used as a trainer, and can be a system expert, but their role here is to advocate for the change and to report on how colleagues are reacting to the change. Super Users also need to do this, but their role has so many other facets. We can see why change agents are such a valuable talent resource for your business; delivering change management is a skill, but we give Super Users those skills and so many more.

Your Super User will act as a change agent at the right stage in the project for you: to plan for the change, to assess the impact, to communicate with your colleagues and feedback to you, they will be involved in business readiness activities and should be trained in change management principles, just like a change agent. Both will help you influence the right behaviours and be a voice for best practice. They will help you gain buy-in by selling the benefits and end vision to your workforce. Both would require ongoing training and support. But ultimately, the change agent is a temporary role, the Super User is a permanent one.

An SME is often suited to be a business process owner, but they are different from Super Users. A Super User is there to influence your end users; your SME can be used to influence your consultants, business analysts or developers. The SME knows the business and understands the technical system solution. A Super User knows the business and they will learn the technical system solution. A Super User becomes an SME, change agent and system expert.

Your SME will know the content well, but likely have no training experience. Your learning and development (L&D) or training team will have the training experience, but likely not the subject expertise. What we are creating with Super Users is someone who has all these skills.

Other names I have come across are champion, ambassador, advocate and evangelist. Even influencer. These are very similar titles as they are there to promote the benefits of your change or product, just like a Super User, but the Super User is all that and a system expert too.

Whatever name you use, we are creating that army of people to help us build success and show the people in our organisation exactly why this system is right for our organisation.

Questions to ask

Do I need system experts to remain in operational teams?
Do I need business process expertise to guide the correct technical solution?
Do I need to embed a digital change and influence best practice usage?
Do I need a large testing and training resource?
If yes, you need a **Super User.**

Do I need to embed cultural change?
Do I need resource to assist with change management activities for a short-term transition?
Do I need advocates to evangelise to business users about the reasons for a change?
If yes, you need a **change agent.**

Do I need a training resource only for the system launch?
If yes, you need a **key user.**

Do I need an industry, product or technology expert for my software engineers and analysts to consult with?
If yes, you need a **subject matter expert.**

Do I need a system administrator role?
If yes, you need a **power user.**

Do I need advanced users to adopt the software whom we can train ourselves?
If yes, you need **citizen developers.** If you don't have standards and governance in place, or mentors to train, you need Super Users to do this.

If you answered yes to all of these, you definitely need **Super Users.**

3   WHAT IS THE ROADMAP FOR USING A SUPER USER NETWORK?

A step-by-step guide for the sequence of activities required for establishing a Super User network, and who should be involved.

When implementing a Super User Model, organisations should use a comprehensive roadmap so that the lead or project team can identify the steps and activities involved in the process. This chapter provides a practical guide to implementing a Super User network for your digital transformation project. With the right roadmap and strategy, your organisation can ensure that your Super User network is implemented successfully and that you are able to maximise the efficiency and productivity of your training and change management initiatives.

Figures 3.1 to 3.4 show the recommended sequence of activities at each phase of your project, and who should be involved in each task. Once you have finished this book, you will understand why each step is important and how it should be executed.

INITIATION PHASE

Figure 3.1 shows the beginning of your project. Your sponsor will approve the business case and begin to form the project team. The first task here is to get buy-in to use a Super User network.
See Chapters 1, 2, 8 and 17 for more details.

PLANNING PHASE

Figure 3.1 shows that you should recruit your Super Users right at the beginning of your project and hold an onboarding event. We can also begin our organisational change management activities. The first task in the planning stage is for your Super Users to contribute to the user requirements for your software.
See Chapters 5 to 9 for more details.

Figure 3.1 Project initiation and planning Super User roadmap

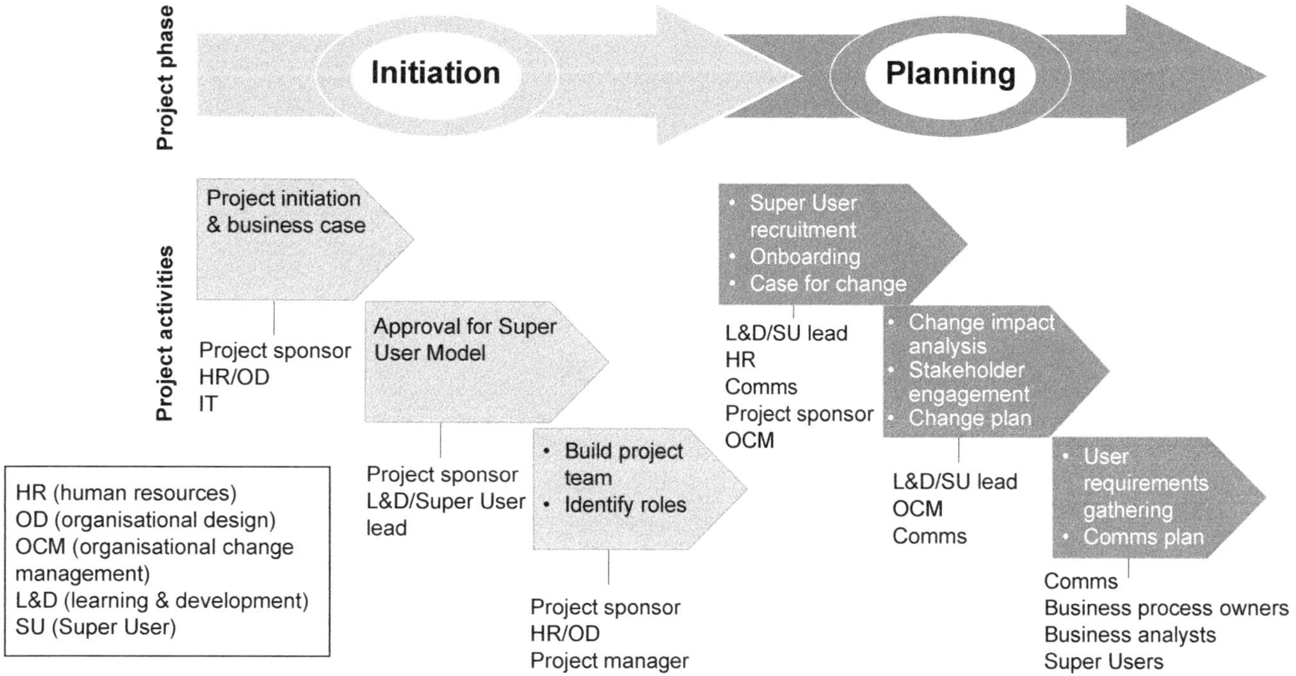

Project phase

Initiation

Planning

Project activities

Project initiation & business case

Project sponsor
HR/OD
IT

Approval for Super User Model

Project sponsor
L&D/Super User lead

• Build project team
• Identify roles

Project sponsor
HR/OD
Project manager

• Super User recruitment
• Onboarding
• Case for change

L&D/SU lead
HR
Comms
Project sponsor
OCM

• Change impact analysis
• Stakeholder engagement
• Change plan

L&D/SU lead
OCM
Comms

• User requirements gathering
• Comms plan

Comms
Business process owners
Business analysts
Super Users

HR (human resources)
OD (organisational design)
OCM (organisational change management)
L&D (learning & development)
SU (Super User)

Initiation and Planning Checklist

☑ Business case for Super Users created with benefits aligned to project vision

☑ Super User network approved as a project resource and permanent operational role

☑ Super User Lead appointed

☑ Super User role profile created

☑ Super User recruitment campaign launched

☑ Super Users selected

☑ Super Users attended onboarding event

☑ Super User Lead has initiated Super User community calls

☑ Super Users and stakeholders attended case for change

☑ Organisational change management lead has started change management activities

☑ Super Users have contributed to software requirements

☑ Super User Lead and internal comms have created a communications plan

BUILD PHASE

Figure 3.2 shows how your Super Users will work with your project team to finalise the design for your build. Super User education can begin with learning the business process designs agreed. Now we know what is being built and how the software will be used, we can start analysing and planning for our training.
See Chapter 4 and Chapter 10 for more details.

TESTING PHASE

Figure 3.2 details how our Super Users and testers begin to get advanced systems knowledge through familiarisation sessions and executing the test plan. Super Users should be involved through each stage of testing as well as validation activities to ensure your data is correct for your live system and all documentation required is present and approved.
See Chapter 4 and Chapter 11 for more details.

Figure 3.2 Project build and test Super User roadmap

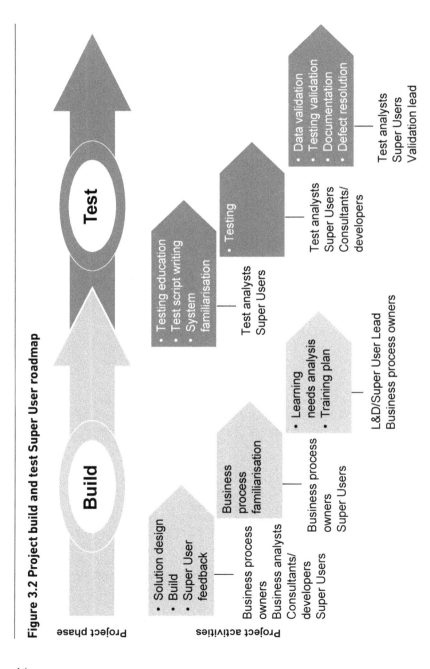

Project phase

Build

Test

Project activities

- Solution design
- Build
- Super User feedback

Business process owners
Business analysts
Consultants/ developers
Super Users

Business process familiarisation

Business process owners
Super Users

- Learning needs analysis
- Training plan

L&D/Super User Lead
Business process owners

- Testing education
- Test script writing
- System familiarisation

Test analysts
Super Users

- Testing

Test analysts
Super Users
Consultants/ developers

- Data validation
- Testing validation
- Documentation
- Defect resolution

Test analysts
Super Users
Validation lead

Build and Testing Checklist

☑ Business process owners and solution developers have solicited feedback from Super Users on the software design, use cases and configuration

☑ Business process owners and business analysts have educated Super Users on the 'To-Be' end-to-end business processes

☑ Training or Super User Lead has conducted the necessary activities to prepare a training plan for approval

☑ Super Users have received basic and advanced system training

☑ Super Users are educated in testing best practice

☑ Super Users have planned the test cases, the testing data required and test scripts are written

☑ Super Users have executed tests, and all appropriate documentation is complete with no critical defects outstanding

☑ Data has been validated by Super Users for migration to the new software

☑ Super Users are confident the business will accept the built software

☑ Super Users are supporting any change management and communications activities

TRAINING PHASE

Figure 3.3 continues Super User education while your project team agree the cutover plan and the rollout strategy. Super Users need to begin building content and practising for the delivery of training to end users. Once the training of end users is completed, and before moving to the next phase, Super Users will comment on the business readiness to transition to putting your software live.
See Chapter 4 and Chapters 10 to 14 for more details.

GO LIVE PHASE

Figure 3.3 ensures the business, and the project is ready to Go Live having met all required deliverables. Cutover tasks are actioned, and internal communication teams generate excitement for the launch. Super Users provide essential support to end users for initial system use, while delivering continuous training interventions.
See Chapters 4, 10 and 14 for more details.

Figure 3.3 Project training and Go Live Super User roadmap

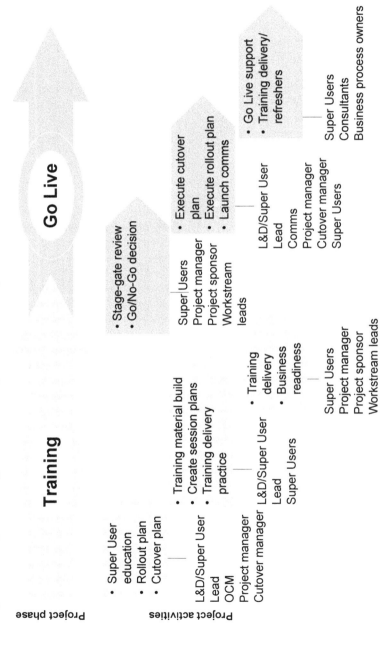

Training and Go Live Checklist

☑ Super Users have attended a train the trainer course

☑ Super User Lead has been consulted on the Go Live rollout plan and cutover plan

☑ Super Users have submitted and practised session plans for end user training

☑ Super Users and the education and training team have developed all required training materials

☑ Super Users have delivered all end user training courses and recorded attendance

☑ Super Users have met all required milestones and deliverables required

☑ Super Users and Super User Lead have given a Go/No-Go decision to confirm opinion on readiness to Go Live

☑ Super Users have completed all cutover activities

☑ Super Users are prepared to actively support end users for an operational Go Live

☑ Super Users are a confirmed step in the end user support model

☑ Super Users have delivered ongoing coaching and training throughout the Go Live period

☑ Super Users are supporting any change management and communications activities, and are attending regular community calls

HYPERCARE PHASE

Figure 3.4 details the importance of evaluation data to assess the success of the project. This includes evaluating the change acceptance using the Prosci® ADKAR Model (awareness, desire, knowledge, ability and reinforcement surveys), the technical system solution, the training effectiveness and the user maturity level. In hypercare we need to ensure the business is ready for the project team to exit by providing training, resolving issues, ensuring process adherence and working as a community to instil best practice and embed continuous improvement (CI).
See Chapters 4, 8, 10 and 15 for more details.

Figure 3.4 Project hypercare and business as usual Super User roadmap

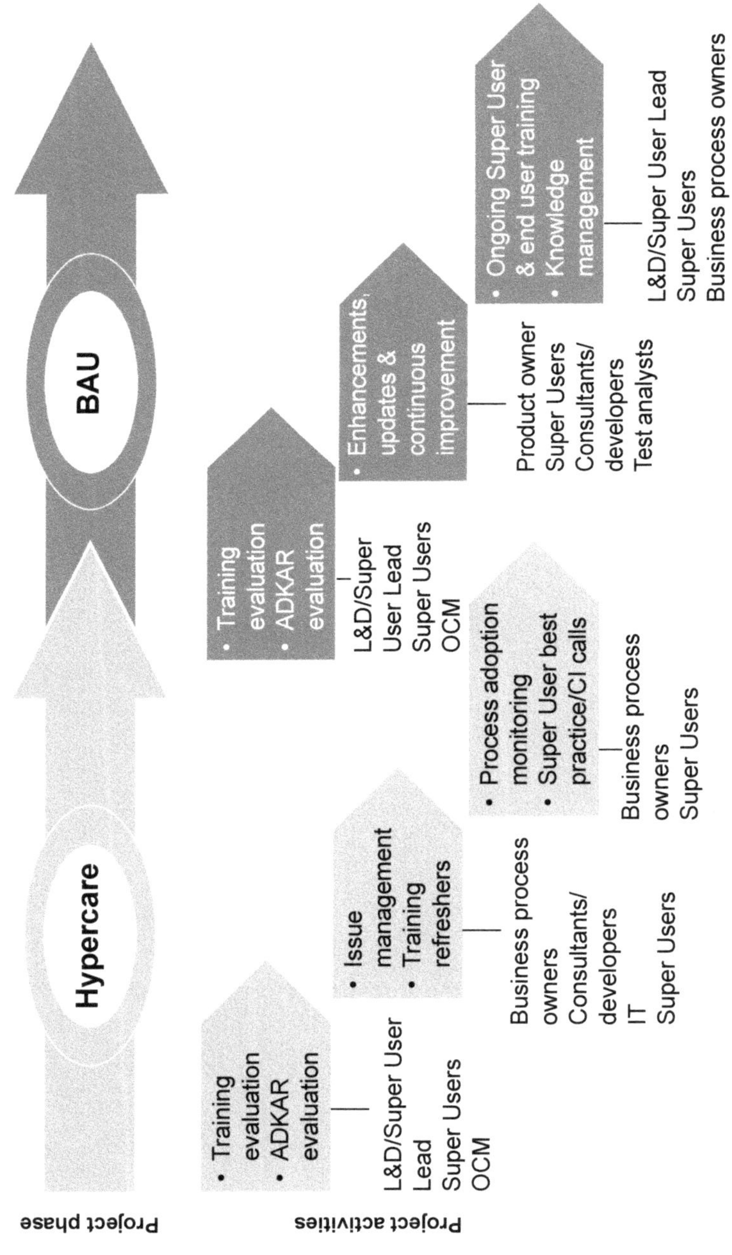

Project phase

Hypercare

BAU

Project activities

- Training evaluation
- ADKAR evaluation

L&D/Super User Lead
Super Users
OCM

- Issue management
- Training refreshers

Business process owners
Consultants/developers
IT
Super Users

- Process adoption monitoring
- Super User best practice/CI calls

Business process owners
Super Users

- Training evaluation
- ADKAR evaluation

L&D/Super User Lead
Super Users
OCM

- Enhancements, updates & continuous improvement

Product owner
Super Users
Consultants/developers
Test analysts

- Ongoing Super User & end user training
- Knowledge management

L&D/Super User Lead
Super Users
Business process owners

Hypercare and BAU Checklist

☑ Super Users have conducted and analysed evaluations to propose recommended next steps

☑ Super Users are liaising with the project team on system tickets and reported incidents

☑ Super Users are reporting on process adoption and key metrics in operational areas

☑ Super Users have confirmed they are comfortable for the project team to exit by ending hypercare

☑ Super User Lead has shifted subject of community calls to discuss continuous improvement in business as usual (BAU)

☑ Super Users are consulted by development teams or product owners to support ongoing system testing and training activities

☑ Super Users are receiving ongoing advanced system training

☑ Super Users have introduced a strategy for regular end user training and knowledge management

☑ Super Users are actively proposing interventions to enhance product adoption based on evaluations of the training, the software, change acceptance and user maturity

BUSINESS AS USUAL PHASE

Figure 3.4 means we continue to work on the actions identified in our evaluation once the system is fully operational to realise full adoption of the software. As time goes on Super Users stay involved by testing, training and communicating about any system changes as well as any required process improvements. Knowledge management and continuous training remains a Super User responsibility for the life of the system. See Chapters 4, 15, 16 and 20 for more details.

The remainder of Part I of the book, as well as Part II, will give you all the detail you need to be able to tick off everything on these checklists.

4   WHAT WILL A SUPER USER DO?...

Providing the reasoning, and the expected benefits, for utilising Super Users through each stage of a digital change project.

Following our chapter on the roadmap you will have a good idea of the activities a Super User can be involved in. I say 'can' as none of this is mandatory: you may want to pick and choose from these sections to suit your project and methodology. However, these are the activities I would propose at each stage of the project, to really make use of their skills and the benefits of having Super Users.

Super Users are going to have an in-depth understanding of the system by the time we are finished with them. They are going to have existing and new world knowledge of the business processes and they are going to know their end users and the day-to-day jobs of the people actually using the system. These things combined are going to add an enormous amount of value at each stage of the project.

Here, we explore in further detail the value added by Super Users from the beginning of the project through to the point when the system is fully operational.

STAGE 1...THROUGHOUT THE PROJECT?

Communication plan

Your internal comms expert will be keeping the business informed as the project progresses and will be building anticipation and awareness. Utilise your Super Users to translate any comms, news or key messages into context related directly to their own department and use your Super Users to keep you informed of how these messages are being received by the business. Listening to your end users is the best way to continually learn, improve by feedback and land your messaging.

Organisational change management (OCM)

Super Users will be key enablers throughout this project; they will help us to engage others in the change, spot change resistance in end users and give them the tools to identify, support and improve on these behaviours. We will educate the Super Users on change management and give them accountability to work on an action plan for each of their own departments or area – supporting them with suggested actions and techniques. This part of the Super User role will be similar to that of a change agent.

You may have an OCM lead: Super Users are there to work with these roles, not replace them. OCM should work with your people managers, the senior executives, and your key stakeholders. Then your Super Users can instead be deployed to influence and support your end users in accepting and embracing the change.

Community

From the initial onboarding activity to business as usual (BAU) we'll be making sure our Super Users take an active part in the community. Attending regular meetings with each other to have their voices heard, to escalate issues, to tell each other system tips or to spur each other on by sharing successes and important news. This is really important to establish at the start of the project and continue throughout the project into the BAU phase. So many Super User programmes disband once into BAU, but this is when this established network of peers sharing best practice, improvement suggestions and working collaboratively will pay dividends, not only to the levels of system adoption but also to the success of your business.

STAGE 2...DURING SYSTEM BUILD?

User requirements gathering

Your Super Users will be a great source of information for your analysts when generating your system requirements document. You may have had a functional one created with IT and solution consultants before you requested bids and quotes from various software providers, but before we build the system to this specification, we need to consider not just the infrastructure and functionality, but the requirements of the business leaders and users. The various Super Users and department leads should consult with your analysts on your requirements documentation to guide you in stating explicitly what the system 'must do'. Or perhaps it is 'should do'. Once you have collated your requirements from Super Users, IT, business leads and some end users, gain consensus to refine your list using the MoSCoW method:

- The system MUST do this.
- The system SHOULD do this.
- COULD the system do this?
- We know the system WON'T do this in this scope, but add it to the future enhancement pipeline.

Business process design

So, we have those expensive consultants, we have developers, we have business process owners and we have system analysts. Why do we need Super Users as well at this stage? Those people we just mentioned absolutely must earn their money here in configuring, designing and producing your ultimate solution, but Super User involvement is still integral at this stage.

You will reap huge rewards by involving Super Users as a sense check against your business process design. How many times have you been involved in previous projects where you have built a system that you are proud to show off, then you provide a demonstration or playback to the business and come away with a long wish list of changes, 'it would be good if' statements, and new requirements to add to your list. So, you either add to your project length by including those new requirements (which may be marginally easier with agile sprints), or you send your project manager back into the lion's den with a declination speech about scope creep, and immediately ensure your business stakeholders feel less excited about the solution they are going to get.

Therefore, it is so important to consult with your Super Users at this stage; they are the ones who will be able to envision how this works out in the real world; they can identify these needs and requirements while you are still in the build stage. Let us not ever forget that a system just enables a user to fulfil a business need for your customer or service, whomever they may be, which could be done with plenty of other systems. So a Super User can help to articulate how your design will best help them to do their jobs to fulfil your business need. It may be that some of these requirements are considered out of scope for your project, but by having Super Users aware of and involved in this decision making, they are able to then confidently explain that back when the same questions inevitably come from the end users or department managers.

Review the business process design, the system look and feel and the intended system configuration with your Super Users during the build phase; let them steer you in the right directions and represent the business users. Identify those awesome changes at this stage while you are better able to do something about them and that will ultimately win over your end users and enhance system adoption in the later stages.

Business process design documents

Once your business process documents are finalised and those consultants and developers are happily building away, we can use these documents as an excellent starting point for educating our Super Users. Before they know the buttons of a system, they need to be familiar with how the end-to-end process should work for your order fulfilment, your logistics execution, your billing procedure, your customer registration process – whatever the process is, we need to know how it **should** work and why, before showing them how to execute it on the system. We'll refer to these documents during testing and for producing training materials, so as soon as they are available, we need our Super Users to be using the business process design documentation to begin their induction to the new system.

Computer systems validation (CSV)

If you are in a pharmaceutical, life sciences, banking, insurance or other regulated industry, you will need to make sure the system you are implementing is a compliant, secure and validated system. As with other sections of this book a Super User can provide a lot of additional support and value, but you should absolutely have a CSV lead on your project to ensure all regulations are adhered to. Use your Super Users here to work with your CSV lead on the documentation. They can give you the expert view to document the risk rating and data integrity. The CSV lead would then need to work with the testing manager and infrastructure lead, ensuring we have adequate technical and functional specifications for the system solution.

I would recommend Super Users be utilised to keep a requirements traceability matrix (RTM) accurate. Ensure each system and user requirement is listed and has a test script written, a business process document, technical specifications, potentially standard operating procedures, and that functional, integration and user acceptance tests are all passed. A large software implementation will inevitably have a huge, but useful, RTM, so asking Super Users to keep it up to date will be a benefit to the project and stage-gates.

STAGE 3...DURING THE TESTING PHASE?

Super Users can often be wrongly associated with being just a training resource, but they are integral to each phase of your project. We discovered in the previous stage why a Super User is crucial at the build phase; next we will look at testing.

I am not here to tell you how important the testing phase is to the success of the project; I know you know this already. But we discuss here some tips on how your Super Users can aid your testing strategy.

Testing team

Your testing team should be experts in the best practice principles of testing code, systems or processes. What they are not experts in, is the day jobs of the end users. Your Super Users can work with your testers to amalgamate all that expertise to ensure our system works for the business.

If you do not have dedicated test analysts, then your Super Users may need testing best practice to be part of their education curriculum. Make sure they know their objective is to find the bugs not pass the tests – more on that later.

Test scripts

You will want to be familiarising your testers and Super Users with the system at the same time, so they can see the step-by-step process that needs documenting into a test script as well as the desired output for each step. If you have a testing team, use them to provide a best practice template for the test script and depending on the number of scripts you need to write, have your Super Users follow this template to write some of the scripts too. I would still recommend having your test scripts approved by a testing expert though.

You need to have a script for every process and every requirement in your initial business requirements documentation. Use the RTM to ensure you have scripts in place for all the likely scenarios for each process and each requirement, and keep Super Users informed or involved in the progress of writing the scripts for each requirement. Listen to your Super Users on what scenarios need testing and what data they need to prove the system is fit for purpose.

Functional testing

Your functional tests can be completed by your testing team, by your analysts or by your consultants. I would recommend though that you have Super Users involved in running some of these functional tests. I am absolutely of the opinion that the best way to have advanced knowledge of a system is to have been involved in testing and seeing how it is meant to work at the fundamental level. It may be an idea to have Super Users involved in retesting after defect resolution at least.

Security testing

Super Users need to be involved in the data collection of existing user roles and system permissions to sense check any future mapping of this and make your testing go a lot smoother. You have this Super User resource to use, so involve them in testing that their own department's role permissions and system access are correct.

Integration testing

If you have a testing team, they absolutely need to play a large part in this as this will be their area of expertise. But I would also recommend that whoever will look after the system in BAU, perhaps your IT helpdesk team, are involved in running integration tests so they will know likely causes and fixes should your system integrations fail at any point in the future. Super Users will gain extensive knowledge in troubleshooting through their involvement in running integration tests. This includes identifying and understanding error messages that may arise when connecting your new system with other systems to exchange data. Integration testing is critical for Super Users to fully comprehend how the system processes work within your wider architecture, providing them with the advanced system understanding we want them to have.

User acceptance testing

Super Users should run the majority of user acceptance testing (UAT) as they know and represent the business. By running all these tests for their relevant areas, they will be fully conversant with how each process is executed by the end of it – enhancing their system knowledge.

I would like to think you listened and had your Super Users involved at the design and build stage, so I am sure there will be no surprises for your Super Users to test here. They should be signing off here on how easy the system is to use – thinking about their end user colleagues. Does it have a logical flow, is the look and feel right, are all drop downs and categories appropriate, is it intuitive, does it follow the process design, does it meet agreed business requirements and is it ready to be passed to the business end users? Stay connected with your Super Users as they conduct these tests and form the answers to these questions – this is going to be insightful as to the level of training end users will need and how easy it is for a new user to pick up and learn.

It is also an idea to expand this stage of testing to other end users and to managers in each business function, but do this only when your Super Users have confidence that the tests are passing. Let your Super Users run the tests first and then pass on to end users for retests or to increase familiarity. Really, you want your project team and Super Users identifying test defects and not your end users, as that can affect the image of the project and the confidence in the solution if the end users come away feeling the system is not functional or desired.

Defect resolution

Your defect log should be transparent to all in the project team, including your Super Users. They can articulate to your developers the importance and priority of fixing each defect and what the adverse effects could be if experienced in real-life usage. Super Users need to be made aware of what the solution was for resolving the defect: was it a system configuration or code change, was it a way of working change or was it simply user error in the first place? This will help them to provide support in the future as they have the knowledge of what can happen if something goes wrong with the system or the way in which a user interacts with it.

Another pet hate creeping into my writing here, and one that should really get a whole ranting chapter of its own, but project managers, please make sure you have a defect resolution stage built into your project plan. Have you ever been on a system implementation that has **not** had defects to resolve? I would guess at no. But how many project plans have you seen that seem to assume every test will pass and you will go straight into end user training after your three-week testing window? You do not want all your tests to be passing, that just means your end users will inevitably experience the bugs and issues after Go Live. A successful testing phase will involve defects found and resolved.

> Make sure you plan a defect resolution stage into your project plan to find them, resolve them and to retest your solutions.

STAGE 4...DURING THE TRAINING PHASE?

We found in previous stages how a Super User resource can deliver lots of value in the build and testing stage of the project, but for the training phase we want them to really shine, as here is where we prove the benefits of your efforts so far.

Super User education

There are two parts to training a system with Super Users, us training our Super Users and them training our end users. Your Super Users will learn such a huge amount about the system if they have been involved in testing, so I hope you take that recommendation. But either way, they need time to practise each process, each screen and familiarise themselves with the system to get to a point where they can confidently, without notes, teach it to someone else.

They also need to learn how to teach – it is not enough to know the system, we need to help them know the best practice ways of rolling it out. So, we will develop them in other ways too: with their confidence, with their delivery skills, with engaging and managing an audience, and with handling change resistance among many other aspects. We will cover the ideal training programme for a Super User in more detail in another chapter, but the time needed to cover all these activities needs to be planned into your project timeline.

Training materials

There are lots of options for training materials that I will write about later, but we need to ensure Super Users are all doing the same thing to the same professional standards. Let your training team provide templates for step-by-step instructions that your Super Users can then populate; provide them with a branded slide deck with learning objectives for their delivery sessions or a full user guide to hand out; help each Super User decide what media, activities or gamification is needed for each session. Your Super Users will write all the technical content for this training material, but they need to be guided on style and best practice by your training lead.

Super Users will need to review and provide acceptance that any media or elearning created by your training team is accurate, and that they can see the benefits. Your Super Users will act as the SMEs to your instructional designers.

End user training

Here is one of the most important activities we needed Super Users for – to deliver systems training to a large group of end users across multiple locations and business functions. But haven't we found already that Super Users can be used for so much more? If you are only using Super Users for this part, you are really missing out on a whole load of benefits.

Your Super Users need to be delivering each course to groups of end users as close as possible to that Go Live date. They may be delivering classroom training, they may be delivering virtually, but they will be running multiple courses and need to be informing the project team of the feedback and questions asked. Your Super Users will all be delivering at the same time, so ensure there are no clashes with room requirements or online schedules, and ensure Super Users feel supported throughout.

Make sure your Super Users are communicating to the business any pre-work or elearning required; ask them to monitor, report on and encourage the completion of this. Your Super Users need to be recording attendance for each delivery session they do, which will be important to business readiness reports as well as to identify if mop-up sessions are needed.

Really motivate and thank your Super Users at this stage; you really could not have done it without them.

STAGE 5...DURING THE CUTOVER PHASE?

The system cutover is a crucial stage in the project and details important activities that are necessary to enable the project to transition from your legacy system, or previous system version, into your new software operations. I can't say enough how Super Users are not just for training. Here is how your Super Users can lead you to a successful rollout during the cutover phase.

Data validation

You have chosen your Super Users as they are the ones who know your business currently. Once they understand the solution, they are best placed to help you translate how your data needs to be mapped into the new software.

Use your project roles in accordance with their expertise. Ensure you have data experts documenting what master data is needed to be loaded into your software before your Go Live to enable the system to function. Your data experts know exactly what fields need to be populated and the configuration required. Your Super Users will add value by sense checking the right data is populated. This could be customer, vendor, regulatory, specification or product data as the most common examples. Your data experts may understand the data infrastructure, but they will not understand the relevance and business application of your data like a Super User would.

The first task for Super Users should be to collate the data required. For example, a list of your suppliers, a list of your customers, or all the relevant product details from your legacy system. This would then be mapped to the relevant new software fields by your data experts. Your Super User may then need to obtain missing data either internally or externally. Once all data is mapped into your new model, your Super Users need to provide approval to confirm that all the data is understood and validated, is being included in the right fields and is being used in the right ways.

There may be other tasks too that a Super User may need to do. We want them to always be thinking of making things as easy as possible for your end users, so at this point they may want to consider communicating what the data will look like in the new system to the business. Perhaps there are new product codes, or a different field name in your new system compared to your old system. We do not need to wait for Go Live to show people this. In fact, your Super Users regularly drip-feeding information such as this to the relevant departments will help to keep your end users and leaders engaged and invested in the new solution. Plus, it means fewer surprises at Go Live as the business users have had more time to consider any implications of the changes, which may in turn feed into your cutover plan; for example, informing suppliers about new purchase order number formats or customers about their new account numbers.

Data migration

Your project and data experts subsequently need to load your mapped and validated data into your new system. This should be part of your testing window, with two test data loads planned, defects captured and potentially space for a third test load depending on the quantity and risk of defects previously captured.

Following each data load your Super User should be required to perform several checks in the new system to check the data has been loaded correctly and completely. Have them check your master data screens to ensure they are populated correctly. Have all rules been followed, for example are your 'bronze' level customers all loaded with 14-day payment terms and your 'gold' customers all with 90 days? Are all your

29

hazardous products loaded with a correct safety data sheet? Are all your high-risk laboratory tests automated to trigger with each product receipt? There will be many more examples of data rules, and these should be agreed and documented beforehand in data migration strategy documentation.

Your Super Users should then re-run some tests using the real data you have loaded (whereas previously you may have used example data in your test system). Your Super Users need to be involved in defect management at this stage, and absolutely listen to them if they say another data load is needed to prove the defect fix has worked or whether seeing the config change is enough for them to feel assured the situation will not reoccur. Project leaders or Super User leaders, we need you to back your Super Users at this stage, trust them and empower them to insist if another test is needed – remember, to get a successful Go Live we need to feel the pain at this point, not after Go Live.

Cutover

You may have a cutover manager at this stage who can be responsible for collating tasks, building your cutover plan, executing the plan in a dress rehearsal run-through and monitoring the execution of the plan at Go Live. This is a joint process and all your project team, department leaders and Super Users need to be involved in a collaborative session to make sure all tasks that need to be completed are included on your cutover plan: with dependencies, ownership, dates, documentation, duration, successor tasks and status included. The cutover plan should be started several weeks in advance, and indeed will need to be if, for example, there are tasks such as external communication to suppliers and customers or communicating a data, expenses or recruitment freeze to the business.

Be aware of your Super User workload at this stage. They do not need to be responsible for completing each cutover task themselves; however, I would recommend they be accountable for the tasks in their relevant areas being completed. Make sure your Super Users know they can delegate a task to a business leader, an end user, an SME or another project team member, but your Super User can again play that go-between role, communicating and chasing up those responsible for the tasks and advising the cutover manager of completion or the need for escalation.

Business readiness

We need a business readiness plan to lay out the strategy for the project to track and measure if the organisation is prepared for a successful Go Live of the new capabilities, and if the business is ready to support the changes after going live. This could be led by a cutover manager, a project manager or your organisational change manager but what I am insistent on is that Super Users have a seat at the table to voice concerns, or give the nod that, yes, their area is fully capable and ready to go.

I have seen a business readiness meeting where the project manager, business process owners and Super Users all told the project sponsor 'no, we would NOT recommend going live at this stage'. Too many tests had multiple repeat defects and were still failing; as a consequence of that the training window had been squeezed too much so that end users felt pressured and were not ready.

As system and project professionals we understand the importance of hitting a Go Live date, of the investment required to date and of the unexpected budget increase involved in an extension. That is internal pain and disruption that should be avoided at all costs. But it is nowhere near as bad as the external pain when a system implementation ends up resulting in delays and issues to your customers, or a hit on profit that impacts on your shareholders.

So when the project sponsor sitting at that table heard the testing team, project managers and Super Users state they recommended a No-Go decision, do we think the project went well when the sponsor insisted on going live anyway? Of course not, it resulted in huge supply chain delays, a massive increase in customer complaints and costs to temporarily revert to a legacy system, all of which exceeded the original budget estimate of a Go Live extension. It did, however, allow me an enjoyable extra three months in a beautiful German village while the solution provider committed to fixing the defects.

STAGE 6...WHEN WE GO LIVE?

We've trained them; we've switched the system on; the new world begins. Your Super Users will not go back to their day jobs until BAU begins and so we need to utilise this resource of experts to support our end users into adopting the system as quickly as possible with minimal disruption experienced. Your Super Users need to be the calming influence in the room, resolving issues quickly and happily championing the new ways of working. They will work seamlessly helping your project team, your IT support teams and your end users to successfully Go Live with your new system.

Go Live support

End users will be reassured to see that there is support in place for those first days; make sure Super Users are strategically spread across locations and departments and let them be the face of your project. Have them there to support the users with that first login, when they think they have forgotten their training (some will have), and have them there to celebrate and congratulate users when they successfully execute their first order or sale or invoice or despatch. If Super Users are there in person, make them identifiable; I've used coloured hats, hairnets and T-shirts before, but if they are online, get the Teams channel ready or send invites for online drop-in sessions.

There will inevitably be some hiccups or issues to escalate back to the project team. Having that network of Super Users as your eyes and ears in the beginning stages will mean you can focus on resolving any issues, getting everyone logged on and operating, and smoothing everything over to get that pat on the back from the project sponsor on a successful launch.

Training

Hopefully you will have conducted your training as close to Go Live as possible, you will have provided end users with training material that they can consult at the point of use and many end users will just be able to crack on and get on with it successfully. But not every end user will have remembered everything from their training, and some may require prompting, one to one coaching or confidence boosting when using the system for those first days and weeks. Your Super Users are there with the system skills and people skills we selected them for and will help each end user in learning as they go, to deliver great business performance and continuity.

Hypercare

You will have agreed a period of time with the business for how long your project team and consultants provide support. Keep your Super Users as the intermediary between the project team and the end users at this stage. The Super Users will be reporting issues to you, and you will be reporting fixes and solutions back to them for them to communicate out. Through their Super User community calls and channels, they will be sharing all this with each other to help everyone develop the knowledge needed to provide support. Your Super Users can begin to transition into their day jobs at this stage, depending on the level of support needed, but keep them involved as the escalation point of contact.

Support model

The Super Users are your front line: they need to be the ones to liaise directly with your end users, provide on-site support, raise any IT tickets and communicate any fixes back to the business – providing that much needed go-between role. Be clear what your support model looks like and communicate to the end users what the triage process is; use emails and posters for visibility of this. I do recommend you avoid the end users speaking directly to IT or to the project team, so you need to ensure they know who to contact. See Figure 4.1 for an example support model.

Figure 4.1 End user issue escalation process

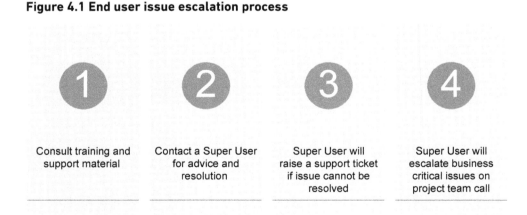

1	2	3	4
Consult training and support material	Contact a Super User for advice and resolution	Super User will raise a support ticket if issue cannot be resolved	Super User will escalate business critical issues on project team call

WHAT WILL A SUPER USER DO?...

Incident resolution

Ensure Super Users attend incident resolution calls with the project team to stay informed on the issues occurring, and to keep managers and end users informed on progress and resolution for their own issues. Hopefully, you will be having two such calls per day, one to review what has been resolved and one to review the new ones that have come in.

Have a monitored chat group within the project team so Super Users can get swift responses to questions: the ones that might not need a ticket raising, but may need clarification, information or a consultant from the team to personally attend to see an issue. Keep your senior project leaders on this chat too; we will want them to react quickly to make sure Super Users are getting the support and quick resolutions that they need to ensure smooth sailing.

Security roles and permissions

Your security and access consultants will have a compliance process established to approve who gets what system permissions, likely after having proof of training and line manager approval. However, I would recommend that this formal procedure does not start until **after** the hypercare period. There may have been issues with people missing from role mapping work, or with training attendance not being reported accurately. If end users need access to keep the business operational, and prevent delays or disruption, trust your Super Users' judgement and grant the access as quickly as you can. You can always run compliance checks to make sure no one has too much access before you move into the BAU phase.

Super Users may also have additional access and permissions in your new system. If this is the case I would recommend the following:

- Consider repudiation (so your Super Users cannot be accused of wrongdoing).
- Document what additional access Super Users have and in what circumstances it should be used.
- Firefighter, or access all areas, role permissions should be given sparingly to Super Users and only granted in cases of crisis management because of a high level of incidents or support requests, and certainly only temporarily.
- Document separation of duties for standard roles: if a Super User is supporting more than one area that causes conflicts, then establish business justification and regular audits.
- Documentation records are recommended to record each time that sensitive access is used.
- Consider a non-disclosure agreement depending on what sensitive data Super Users can see.
- Consider these high levels of access being granted to support hypercare only, rather than leaving them with higher permissions permanently.

- Initiate self-audits – to ensure we have audit trails of whenever the team use access in live systems to make data changes.

Key performance indicator reporting

Establish reporting dashboards on incident analysis, sharing with all on the team, and indicate how many system issues we are having and how we are performing against targets to resolve incidents. Monitor the operational activities, for example production, quality, goods-in, invoices, orders and planning, to ensure the outputs are remaining within acceptable levels and not suddenly declining, indicating further support is needed. Present key metrics for the output of the business function and compare this to the levels before the project – although, allow for the learning curve (see Figure 4.2), as people will be slower doing something new at first until they progress through the competency levels. (**See Chapters 10, 14 and 15 for more on the Three E's of Competency**).

Figure 4.2 Learning curve and the Three E's of Competency (Source: Image adapted from Complex Learning Curve in an article by Disha Gupta (2022) *The learning curve theory*. WhatFix. https://whatfix.com/blog/learning-curve/)

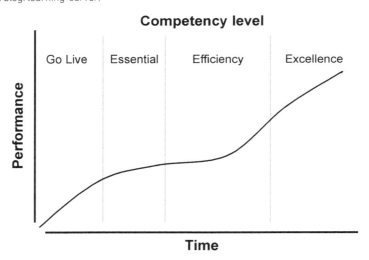

Process adoption monitoring

Ask your Super Users to present to the project team and business leaders, at least weekly, on how they feel their dedicated business area is adapting to the change and to the new ways of working.

- How much additional training is being delivered?
- Are they seeing the desired behaviours?

- Provide commentary on process adherence.
- Report on errors seen – how many are user errors? Are these as a result of further training being required or other reasons?
- Provide information on any delays or bottlenecks seen.
- Report on status of any refresher training or mop-ups.

Transition from hypercare to business as usual

Hypercare will have been planned for a specific amount of time. If we are not seeing a reduction in incidents, and a positive response on process adoption by the end of this period, then your project leaders need to extend the hypercare end date, and be prepared to provide extra resources to accelerate support so that we can transition to business as usual, handing over issues to IT and to Super Users only when at a manageable level.

Above all, I hope a celebration is planned for your Super Users and project team after this stage: they deserve it.

STAGE 7...WHEN WE MOVE INTO BUSINESS AS USUAL?

In stages 1–6 we looked at the role we feel the Super Users should play throughout the build, test, training and Go Live stages of your project. You will know I say this a lot, but the Super User is there for the life of your system, not the life of your project. Your project team may move on at this point as your existing IT teams take on the support for the system, but your Super Users remain the go-to resource for your end users long after Go Live. This also means you need to ensure your project sponsor or project manager agrees to be accountable to ensure the activities below are managed and that they remain committed to having Super Users.

System adoption

We have done everything right up to now but if we walk away at the point of the BAU transition, we are abandoning the crucial stage of system adoption. Make sure your legacy system is turned off and monitor usage of the new system to make sure your investment is being used for the benefits you planned. If the system you implemented is the only way to perform their day jobs, then you still need to monitor how it is being used, for example are we seeing user errors or breakpoints? How many support requests are your Super Users or helpdesk receiving? Analyse and measure these to learn from.

If you are noticing intervention is needed, then you can use your network of Super Users not only to highlight this to you, but also to keep offering training to the end users and to cascade messages of how important a specific way of working is. Super Users should remain an example of best practice usage; hold them to high standards and continue to publicly call their successes out, thus encouraging others.

Super Users are a tool for you to use to enhance adoption of your new system, through continual support and training, but it's my opinion that the people managers are ultimately accountable for driving new behaviours.

In the days of big data and insight-driven decision making, it is not enough to allow people to operate the way they always did. You invested in this system for a reason, and you need to continually drive this, way after Go Live.

For example, I have seen a business that launched a system for sales forecasting that became optional in a few teams (not all – so inconsistently), despite us advising it was mandatory during the training stages. This was simply because the team manager only cared if they hit their sales targets each month and didn't drive for them to use the system to aid this, or to consider the future potential of how many more sales they could have, or the insights we could get from the data. This needed addressing at a senior level between the sponsor and the leader of the relevant business function, to have that mandatory versus optional conversation. Managers should drive the change; we just might need to drive them to do that.

Role of project team and product owner

Although your project team may move on, it is likely you will have a product owner or a team of developers in place to look after the system, plan enhancements, future development sprints or cloud updates from the system provider. Having Super Users in place helps the product owner as they have testers, feedback mechanisms and methods to cascade communication about changes and ways of working. Use your Super Users to train your end users in these changes, thus providing continual education.

End user training

Your Super Users should remain in place as your dedicated training resource for new people, as well as providing upskilling and refresher training to your existing team. Managers should be committed to using the Super User to train a new colleague on the system, so everyone receives the same consistent message from the experts. New people should not be left to be trained by other end users who will still have a varying level of skill and knowledge. Use only those who have the system skills and training strengths: your Super Users.

Training materials

Particularly with updates, interface changes and your own enhancements, you will likely see your original training materials become outdated. You have the option here to enable Super Users to update them themselves or to alert your education or L&D team to the need to do so. Either way, ensure you have version control in place and use Super Users, as well as any document management or learning management system, to ensure end users and new starters are using the current version of any training resource. Leaving these documents to become outdated will affect the reputation of your training team and means any new colleagues will experience a less effective and more frustrating method of learning the system. If left to continue this will adversely affect best practice usage over time.

Knowledge management

Like with training materials, you need a strategy to consider knowledge management. Where will users go to receive just in time training support available to them quickly at the point of use? Can users add questions, tips of their own, or create their own 'How-To' guides? All of these are great ideas to pursue, but ensure Super Users have the responsibility to oversee any content created for accuracy and consistency, and that they address any questions or comments received. Knowledge management will be covered in more detail later.

Sustaining the community in BAU

You can expect a certain turnover and attrition with Super Users, so someone needs to monitor a list to ensure that the support and training resource remains in place. Ask managers to inform you when a Super User leaves and that a nomination happens for their next Super User. Although, depending on the level of support needed by then, it could be that they can be supported by other Super Users – but you need to keep an eye on the coverage you have. You will need to onboard and train your new Super Users, though with a lesser version of the programme your original Super Users had.

Someone needs to continue the regular community meetings you had, perhaps less often, but Super Users still need a mechanism to share feedback, tips and suggestions with each other. This empowers each of them personally to drive improvements for business processes and keeps system adoption and best practice usage as a topic of conversation. You need to agree in advance who will own this community to ensure these activities still take place.

Your product owner and training team need to ensure your Super Users stay as advanced users, by continually providing training and demonstrations to them. Hold your Super Users to account by making sure they cascade this out to all. This should not be optional – Super Users are there to increase the capability of your end users.

Your Super Users can also be considered as a talent pool; keep them informed of personal development and progression opportunities as part of their reward and recognition for their efforts. You have here a group of engaged and talented people; do not let that slide.

PART II
IMPLEMENTING A SUPER USER NETWORK
'The How'

- Develop a recruitment strategy to source suitable candidates for the Super User role.

- Establish a comprehensive job description for the Super User position, outlining the key responsibilities, required skills and performance expectations for the role.

- Utilise best practices to foster a collaborative and engaged community of Super Users.

- Create a change management plan that outlines the steps needed to enhance acceptance of the change and facilitate adoption of the technology.

- Generate a communication plan for the software project to meet stakeholder requirements and highlight the value of Super Users.

- Analyse learning needs and create a formal training plan for stakeholders' approval.

- Develop an education and upskilling programme for Super Users that aligns with the software project's goals.

- Utilise a recommended session plan for a train the trainer course to enhance the confidence of Super Users in delivering software training.

- Apply best practices in learning design to create digital learning materials that increase the likelihood of software adoption and facilitate strong system knowledge in end users.

- Deliver effective training sessions by utilising recommended tips that are specific to learning new software.

- Evaluate the effectiveness of training programmes by assessing user competency, software suitability and organisational culture.

- Integrate Super User tasks and responsibilities into the software development life cycle to continue to demonstrate the value of using a Super User resource.

5 HOW DO WE RECRUIT AND SELECT OUR SUPER USERS?

Detailing the recommended recruitment, selection and onboarding strategy.

In Chapter 1 we discussed the case for having them, but who should we ask to be Super Users and how many do we need?

Once we have senior executive level commitment to a Super User programme that lasts throughout the software rollout phases into business as usual operations, we can begin the process of finding Super Users. We have three options: (1) use data and insights to find them, (2) ask leaders to nominate people and (3) ask for volunteers.

My preference is that you do it in that order: try identifying them first, then ask for nominations based on already identified talent and a role profile, and lastly ask for volunteers where you have gaps. Either way it should be done with the colleague's agreement; they should never be **told** to take on this role.

HOW MANY SUPER USERS DO WE NEED?

Table 5.1 describes the ratio of Super Users required to the number of end users. Complexity means how easy the system is to use compared to old ways of working, and effort is the amount of resource and materials required to train your end users.

This is a guideline for you, and you may want to take into consideration other factors such as team size or geographical location. It may be simpler to say one Super User per team or department.

Table 5.1 Super User to end user ratio

	Low complexity	Medium complexity	High complexity
Low effort	Not required	1:100	1:60
Medium effort	1:60	1:40	1:40
High effort	1:40	1:40	1:20

If you are having Super Users, you will also need to have a position of Super User Lead or your training, OCM or L&D teams should take ownership of the network.

IDENTIFICATION CRITERIA

Work with HR and use data and insights to find the right people for your project. Consider activities in the following order:

1. Who is in the right geographical location?
2. Who has the right business process knowledge and experience in current or previous roles or has done a similar role in a previous project?
3. Who has high ratings in your performance management system or talent matrix?
4. Who has high system usage or activity?

When you get this far, and you have names from this exercise, get them on your list quick before other projects take them.

NOMINATIONS

With the help of your internal communications expert draft up a role profile tailored to your organisation and ask the managers for nominations of people who fit this. The request should go out to all people managers and function heads, asking for nominations and describing the role in detail. At this stage, all people managers should be aware of the name and objectives of your project through your comms plan, so this should not be news to them, but ensure your comms explains to them how critical the role of Super User will be to the success of the rollout and system adoption. Invite questions from the managers but do monitor responses and chase up people for their nomination if needed.

After the nomination process the Super User Lead or training team has an onboarding conversation with this colleague to agree they are the right fit and know what they are signing up to. Communicate this as a real compliment to the colleague that they have been nominated and give them the role profile to read; it is important they know what they are committing to. I have rarely encountered people not wanting to take on this role, but if so, a conversation should take place with the manager to ask for another nomination or to see if they want to ask for volunteers. After accepting the Super User role, advise the colleague you will be in touch for onboarding to the community and to commence their training.

I prefer to go with talent identification and nominations first as we want the **best of the best** to be Super Users, the people in the teams who already have potential, who are already the go-to people. We want the people who managers have identified as talent who should be developed, or the ones who stand out themselves for having ambition, influence and drive.

VOLUNTEERS

It is likely that after this process, you will have gaps across the organisation that you need to analyse and identify. It is at this point we can advertise for volunteers who can be vetted.

With the greatest respect I do not recommend just asking for volunteers first. We do not want the people who just want a break from their day job; we want the people who love their day job and want to help make it better. We also do not want to hear from managers that they are nominating someone who needs the experience, or to see if they are up to it, or because they need to improve their performance by stretching themselves. By doing it by nomination process first with a desirable role profile, we avoid a lot of this. I've had very few difficult conversations with volunteers in the past, and it is hard, as you don't ever want to discourage someone from developing themselves. But on occasion for the good of the project if I haven't been fully convinced by the choice of a Super User, I have either addressed it with the manager or asked for two Super Users for that particular area.

Your call for volunteers needs to be engaging and informative. The project or the new system would ideally be known to colleagues at this stage through your comms plan, but you may need to provide more information about it as this role advertisement will need to go to all colleagues using a medium you know is likely to reach everyone, and a headline likely to attract attention. Provide a link to the role profile with your advertisement and a deadline for applications. Discuss with the manager in each area who to select from the applications you have had, and ensure an onboarding conversation takes place either with you or with their manager.

It may be that you have no ideal nominations or volunteers after these stages, so I would recommend then working with the manager for that particular area and with HR to see who could be asked. On some occasions, Super Users can be moved to look after teams they don't necessarily work with now; it could be they have previous or transferable experience, but I am confident that after these activities you will have your list of Super Users to onboard.

TIME NEEDED FOR ROLE

As soon as your project initiation and business case is completed and you have decided on your project team, we then move to recruit our Super Users. We need support from the sponsor and C-suite executives to ensure we do not encounter resistance from people managers not wanting to release their best people to the project. It needs to be communicated that freeing them up completely is essential to achieving both the project and organisational objectives.

Super Users need to work with your process experts and consultants on your design in the build stages; they need to be involved in testing; they need to receive training themselves; and then they need to train the end users in the ways of working in advance of your Go Live date. Plan your programme of events for Super Users to coincide with this and you can make sure you are recruiting at the right time.

There is no model or rule for this, but an estimate will be that Super Users will spend the proportions of their time on project activities as shown in Table 5.2.

Table 5.2 Super User time commitment by project stage

Project stage	Time commitment
Build stage	20–50%
Testing stage	50–100%
Training stage	100%
Go Live	50–100%
Hypercare	50–100%
Business as usual	10–20%

I have seen rollouts with Super Users full-time and their day jobs backfilled, and I have seen scenarios where they still do their day jobs and commit a day a week to the project. You know your project best and will have to make this decision accordingly. If it is a substantial change with a big testing and training resource required, we need a full-time project secondment role and would be more likely to want as much of their time as we can obtain.

VARIETY OF ROLES

We want a variety of roles as Super Users, from entry level to experienced professionals to the middle manager hierarchy too. A Super User from one area could be a manager, and in a similar department it could be someone in a junior position, as long as they fit the role profile. But ideally you will have this mix for Super Users to really benefit from their own network. You certainly do not want all managers, but if a manager cannot think of the ideal nomination or fits the profile best themselves for their knowledge, then we do want them. You also don't want too many people from one area; I've had managers before nominate nearly all their team, wanting them to have advanced training. If this occurs you just need to reassure the manager they will all get the training they need and make them aware of the time commitment for a Super User. We don't want to wipe out their resource completely and, besides, actually less gets done like that as too many Super Users in one area results in no ownership.

You may need to make your own suggestions to get the mix that you need, or to ask for two Super Users per area. Keep checking your list ensuring you have good coverage of roles, areas and expertise. When you end up with this mix, we want to make it clear to all of them that there is no rank among Super Users. Each Super User will be asked to do certain activities such as testing or training people, and **all** Super Users will do that. Managers in a Super User role will not be there just to be involved in the decision making for their area; they will be training their own area too.

REWARD AND COMPENSATION

If the extent of your project identifies the need for a full-time role, which I would recommend, you will need to work with HR on a secondment role, so the business can backfill them to free them up completely. This secondment will need to be attractive enough to appeal to the best of the best, as well as work within your existing pay grades structure. Usual rules apply: people on higher wages will not get a pay cut but it may mean you compensating other people more to ensure we can use their valued expertise. HR will need to consider the costs of project secondment salaries, and for the temporary backfilling of their roles, as part of the budget calculations. HR needs to be insistent with the sponsor that not backfilling the Super Users could cause a significant risk to the project; the Super Users need to be able to commit fully to the project and not be disrupted with demands from their original role.

But there are many ways to reward a Super User. Consider bonuses and financial incentives to completing project stages on time; consider covering travel costs or an entertainment budget they would not normally get in their day jobs. One of the most successful Super User programmes I have seen involved rewarding the colleague by promising (and delivering) additional training and development to aid them in future career progression. (They were already being fairly compensated though, let me add; as much as your company and shareholders deserve profit, your people deserve a living wage too.)

ONBOARDING

As soon as possible after finalising your list of Super Users, we need to provide an onboarding activity. This should include more detail on the project vision, the selected system, any change management output, some team bonding activity, and reviewing the Super User role profile and activities in detail with them. More details will come in a later chapter but we're going to use this session as a great start to creating a team of engaged and enthusiastic Super Users, all committed to using their expertise to enact the future utopian vision for the project and the organisation.

Questions to ask:

How many end users do you have?
How complex is the system compared to current ways of working?
How much effort is required to train the new solution and create training materials?
Using the **ratio table**, you can now calculate the number of Super Users needed.

Do I have data on individuals with high performance ratings and talent grid positions?
Do I have data on who has previous software project experience?
Do I have data on current system usage, competency level and accuracy?
Your HR, talent and IT professionals can now give you a list of **suggested people** for Super Users.

Do I have project sponsor and HR backing to create project secondments and backfill roles?
Do I have a Super User role profile? (See Chapter 6).
Do I have project FAQs?

Do I have a creative comms campaign articulating who we want as Super Users?
You can now approach people managers to ask for Super User **nominations**.

Is the organisation aware of the project and the vision?
Do I have a communications channel that can reach all impacted people?
Do I have a creative comms campaign?
You can now request **volunteers** for the Super User role.

Do I have gaps in Super User coverage, per departments and business functions?
Do I have gaps in experience or influence?
You can now work with HR and department heads to **approach people directly** about the opportunity.

Do I have secondment contracts in place?
Do I have the necessary detail on the project and new software?
Do I have project sponsor commitment to attend?
You can now organise your Super User **onboarding event**.

6 WHAT DOES A SUPER USER ROLE PROFILE LOOK LIKE?

A template for a Super User role profile.

Work with your project team, HR and internal communications experts to draft a role profile that fits your organisation and project aims. An example is shown below. The role profile should ideally contain your project branding and identity, so they can easily link it to what the project or system is about. You could provide project FAQs at the same time as the profile to ensure people are aware of the key objectives.

Role HR specifics

- full-time role or proportion of time given to role;
- estimated length of commitment;
- reward or compensation if applicable;
- location if different;
- reporting lines;
- deadline for applications or nominations.

Key messaging

- How critical this role is to the success of the project.
- Articulate how we are looking for the best of the best.

Desirable skills

- experienced and influential member of the team;
- excellent IT skills (add name of new system for those who may have previous experience);
- expert knowledge of existing processes in own area;
- confidence to learn how to deliver training and present to colleagues;
- reliability at meeting deadlines and working on own initiative;
- excellent communication and interpersonal skills.

Accountabilities and project activities

- Be an advocate for the change.

- Cascade communications and project news to your teams.
- Be an ambassador for the project and a positive influence on end users to promote the value of the system.
- Consult with the project team on the system and business process design.
- Prepare relevant test scripts and data to test the business process on the system.
- Run testing and record system defects.
- Work with the project team on monitoring and resolving defects.
- Take an active part in the Super User training programme.
- Develop advanced skills at using the system.
- Work with the L&D or education team to produce training material and activities.
- Promote and monitor completion of any digital learning or pre-work.
- Drive your colleagues to take essential key steps for success at cutover stage.
- Schedule and deliver end user training courses and demonstrations.
- Ensure training resources are planned, booked and prepared for training delivery.
- Support end users with questions, troubleshooting and issues at Go Live.
- Liaise between end users, IT and project team when escalation is required.
- Support IT and the project team with other tasks as required.
- Own and update training materials to document procedures and step-by-step instructions.
- Manage training documents and version control in the nominated knowledge base.

Future duties

- Continue to influence best practice and adoption of the system.
- Systems champion or go-to person in resident area.
- Coach and mentor colleagues as required.
- First escalation point before the IT helpdesk.
- Share system tips among colleagues and the Super User community.
- Arrange and conduct regular training sessions for own area (new starters, process changes and skills improvement).
- Continuous improvement activities as required.
- Systems testing as required for future system enhancements.
- Maintain accurate documentation of ways of working, procedures and training material.
- Deliver training for new features, enhancements and changes.

- Maintain links and communication between the Super User community, the training team and the system product owner(s).

Adapt this as required, but I would recommend each of these sections need to be present, to say who we want, what they will do in the project and what we expect of them once back in their day jobs. This is what needs to be agreed by your senior executives and people managers before the recruitment process; a Super User remains in place for as long as your system does.

When choosing your Super Users, you should look for people with effective communication and teaching skills as they will greatly influence whether the solution is ultimately accepted or rejected by the users. An aptitude for leadership is especially important, as end users can often resist change or struggle to learn new technology. Communications, planning and good training are all essential for system adoption, but so is ensuring end users are supported after the initial Go Live.

Furthermore, Super Users need the technical ability not only to learn the system well enough to train it, but also to properly identify issues and bugs. They need to be able to troubleshoot on the systems, identify process improvements and work with the project team on the urgency and importance of resolving any bugs. Therefore, being IT or digital savvy to begin with always needs to be a desirable skill, even though the system may be new to them or that we intend to train them on it anyway.

7   HOW CAN WE CREATE A SUPER USER COMMUNITY?

Methods and advice for how to establish a community culture for your Super User network, and why this is necessary.

Why do we need our Super Users to function as part of a community?

Because to execute an end-to-end business process – the purpose of your business – typically involves multiple departments. Because it encourages cross-functional working. Because it enables Super Users to learn from each other, share best practice and benefit from being part of a network of engaged professionals.

ONBOARDING

We need to create an onboarding event for your Super Users to begin with; I would really recommend you give this the time it needs, and do it face to face.

Start the event with a welcome and a thank you from the most senior person involved in your project, the sponsor or a member of your board. Ensure they articulate the vital role a Super User can play and how they can influence the success of the project. The project sponsor should describe the future vision of both the business strategy and how your new system will contribute to this strategy. Encourage questions from your Super Users at this point before letting your senior person go. Try do this informally, maybe over a good old cup of tea and biscuits.

Facilitate a discussion among your Super Users over the current state and the future state (As-Is/To-Be) and have them raise the points of why we need to change. Ask them to produce a five-point plan for how they reach the future state: start with 'If I was CEO I would...'. This helps them to think about how change is needed and desirable. Another exercise to do to bring Super Users together with a common goal is to ask them to come up with their own mission statement to represent the Super User group.

I would recommend some 'getting to know you' activity. It could be as simple as everyone introducing themselves and doing the old 'interesting fact' thing that everyone loves in these settings, right? You could use icebreakers such as discussing the guest list for their fantasy dinner party, or split them into groups with the objective to find one thing in common with each other, as well as have a few moments to chat.

We need to provide a presentation or handout detailing the full role profile and expected responsibilities for the Super Users; let them see the journey ahead and ask questions about it. It is a good idea to let the group agree a team charter, or ground rules, agree the levels of contact with each other, the promise to share tips and what works well with each other, and other rules the group may come up with that will aid collaborative working and mutual respect.

It is a good opportunity here to enable Super Users to meet other project team members, or at least be informed of the organisational structure in the project and who they will be working with.

Finally, if you are ready at this point, even if it is just a video, it would be ideal for them to see a demonstration of the system. There is more you can put into your onboarding event though: tailor it to your needs and what you want to get out of the day.

If your budget allows it, treat them to a meal or a few drinks out at the end of the day. We all know this is where the real team bonding occurs.

COMMUNITY CALLS OR MEETINGS

We need all Super Users to attend meetings on a regular basis, in person if you are in the same location but more likely on a virtual meeting. The frequency will change depending on the stage of your project and the level of activity. For example, fortnightly is enough during a long build or testing stage, more often if deadlines are pending. A daily call would be encouraged while they are actively training end users or at Go Live. Once you are comfortably into BAU, I would move the calls to quarterly.

Try to encourage a rota of hosts, so it feels more that they are participating and leading the agenda themselves rather than having to just attend something. Get an agenda out in advance so people know what to expect and if they need to prepare anything. Use this call to ask for progress updates on actions. Make sure there is a point in the call for an open floor discussion for anyone to voice feedback, challenges or questions. Have a regular slot to share what has been working well, what tips they can offer each other, system tips or otherwise. If you are in BAU use it as an opportunity to continue demonstrating advanced uses of the system, troubleshooting techniques or new features. Ensure you finish with a call to action: have they any other actions to do next or are there updates to inform their teams about back in the business? We need them to make sure they agree to go back to their teams and provide a system demonstration for anything new that has come up in the call. Provide recordings to anyone who missed the call and give them those same actions.

PROBLEM SOLVING

Either call ad hoc meetings to address any issues raised or have a regular agenda item in your community calls to discuss process improvements. Try not to intervene too much and allow the solutions and discussions to come from the group – for example, if there is a bottleneck issue raised by one department just facilitate the discussion with the relevant Super Users to enable them to make their own suggestions on how things can be improved, or how the issue can be resolved. Here is where the work you have put in for team bonding and cross-functional collaboration will show its value.

WHAT'S IN IT FOR ME?

We need to provide added bonuses for being Super Users: the reward for their extra effort. I can recommend many ways to do this. Advertise networking opportunities to the group, internal or external. Recommend personal development resources to them or put them in touch with mentors throughout the business. If there are spaces available on one of your L&D-led training courses, offer them to the Super User group first. Is there an opportunity for someone to present something to a senior director or board member – ask for volunteers from the group giving them those career progression opportunities they may not have had before. Do you get perks you can raffle off to the group? Gig or theatre tickets for example? Is there something in the budget so you can offer them social activities – not mandatory of course. What do they get for being a Super User that they would not have had if they had remained in their previous positions in the business?

EMPOWERMENT

Thinking back to how we got the Super Users because we wanted the best of the best from each department or function, encourage them to act on their own initiative. Empower them to make suggestions, to trial ideas, to present solutions to the business – trust their decision-making judgement. We want Super Users to be keeping you informed, but they are in place for their expertise, so we want to empower them to do their best for the business and for your people in the way that they feel is best.

ACCOUNTABILITY

It can affect engagement if there is a disparity apparent between the workload of Super Users. Ensure Super Users all agree, perhaps in the beginning with your team charter, with the activities they will commit to, even when in business as usual. I would recommend an objective be given to Super Users relating to ongoing training, knowledge management and continuous improvement so that their performance against the objective can be reported on and tracked by line managers. However, to enhance community cohesion, call it out in meetings if one Super User is busier than another and request support from other community members to assist them. Escalate this as a formal request to line managers if needed.

SOCIAL ACTIVITIES AND TEAM BONDING

Social activities help with team relationship building and cohesion, and provide rewards and a great employee experience. I feel this is so crucial to success it should be planned in. Engaged employees enjoy their work, see the purpose in it and feel personally responsible for ensuring success.

Create a social calendar for Super Users and the full project team, create getting to know each other events, host a Friday happy hour with no discussion of work allowed, create fun and interesting activities in the work environment. Due to geography or childcare as well as personal preference, there needs to be a mix here of online, inside and outside work activities. Plan nights out as well as lunch break outings. Encourage people to put their work aside for short periods to come and mingle over coffee, doughnuts or pizza. For remote teams, organise virtual team activities to explore each other's working style more; I like PRINT and Insights Colour Model for this as they remain business focused while still enabling a more personal glimpse into our individual strengths and differences.

SOCIAL MEDIA AND COMMUNICATION STRATEGY

Social network platforms should play an important part in your Super User community strategy, as indeed with your project team. We need to be thinking here about tools such as: Teams, Slack, Yammer, Workplace, RingCentral, SharePoint, Confluence or other alternatives. We need a way to encourage sharing of information between the community, as well as for the project to inform and update the Super Users.

Working with your internal comms team, agree this strategy up front. Whichever of the above tools you use or have available to you, you need to consider how they will be used. How will you differentiate or highlight important updates in between general chat – do you have a way to favourite or pin important posts or will you have two channels, one for things that may need to be referred to and one for chat and questions. Encourage your Super Users to use the channel for questions and answers – a way for Super Users to seek support or clarification from each other or from the project team.

Your comms plan should have your Super Users registered as a group of stakeholders to be communicated to – share important news and milestones with them, keep them involved by giving them a view of the same updates that went to the board, write about the successes of the project or the feedback from end users. Use these ideas in your comms plan to ensure you have a regular flow of internal communications into this channel and I believe this will help to keep motivation and engagement high.

Your project team will need to be advised to regularly share information into your chosen Super User channel too. Ensure they share links to important documents, advise them of important fixes or maintenance windows, advertise significant changes or improvements and importantly get the project team to call out and thank Super Users for particular tasks. Doing this publicly in such a way for all Super Users to see can be a real boost.

Ask your Super Users to drop a note into the group after significant activities: have they just spent a full day at a particular site or delivering a particular course or learning a new topic? Then ask them to ensure they update the group at the end of the day with some feedback. The Super User Lead may need to instigate this at first but once some start doing it, this should encourage other Super Users to start doing it organically.

Your chosen social media channel should also be used for, funnily enough, being social. Again, you may have to start this off for them, but once they see the precedent it should continue naturally. Is one of your Super Users expecting a baby? Put a congratulations notice in the group (with permission). Follow up and ask how your colleague's exciting weekend plans went. Has one of your Super Users returned from a dream holiday?

Get them to share some photos (not all of them – no one wants to see that). Keeping these personal touches as an important part of the group will help to strengthen the bonds and feel more like a community of engaged colleagues from different areas of the business who care about each other, and feel personally invested in wanting to help each other. This can be just as useful as sharing the news of that long-awaited defect fix.

You may also want to consider an out of work chat. One that cannot be mandatory of course but can be suggested and set up by you. This will have a work benefit of ensuring your Super User chat does not get overwhelmed by the sharing of memes and gifs. An outlet for humour is important, so providing an alternative means of doing that can help to keep your work social media channel business focused. It is inevitable these days for this way of communicating to happen, so give them a way of doing this. Again, it will strengthen their relationships as a community of colleagues, but it also may give them an opportunity to blow off steam and let them have a moan with each other away from the pressures of work. WhatsApp, Telegram and Signal are good external chat options. One last disclaimer on this, you will need to make sure colleagues are aware of your social media policy too: it may be an out of work chat not controlled by the business, but they need to be aware that anything offensive posted can have consequences.

Finally, encourage your Super Users to post onto LinkedIn. This has several benefits: it helps your organisation to look like a great and professional place to work and it will help to enhance the network and reputation of your Super User colleagues. Ask them to share successes and updates on their LinkedIn posts; ask them to share thanks and praise with their colleagues; ask them to share their tips for the system you are using or for the project methods in implementing them.

Ask them to post about this book too.

Checklist

- ☑ Onboarding event hosted

- ☑ Super user team charter agreed

- ☑ Social evening event arranged

- ☑ Community calls established with rota and agenda agreed

- ☑ Training for continuous improvement and problem solving agreed for post-Go Live

- ☑ Professional and personal development strategy and techniques agreed

- ☑ Teams channel created for information sharing, questions and knowledge management

- ☑ Team chat created for general conversations

- ☑ Social events planned (virtual, out of work time and within work time)

- ☑ Objectives written for individual performance reviews

- ☑ Talent retention and career development strategy agreed

- ☑ Succession planning strategy agreed

- ☑ Copy of this book purchased for each Super User

For more tips on sustaining the Super User community, see Chapter 26.

8 HOW DO WE DEVELOP A CHANGE MANAGEMENT PLAN?

A methodology to follow to execute a comprehensive organisational change management strategy for your software project.

In the name of being thorough I will document here what a complete change management plan could look like for your software project. Please do your research, employ organisational change management experts and adapt this as suits for your organisation. The Super Users will not need to be involved at every stage of this, and certainly should not be leading it, but will add valuable contributions to the outcomes if involved at key points.

Ideal change management activities for a software implementation project include the following.

Business case

Your project sponsor and team will document the justification for the project, the expected costs, return on investment (ROI) and the expected benefits for your new or upgraded software. We will need to refer back to this throughout the project to ensure what we build meets these objectives, and that our operational software realises the benefits.

Project initiation

Work with your project manager and project sponsor to understand your business case and have a change initiation meeting with the top-level executives. At a high level, the change and objectives need to be described and the roles or business functions that will be impacted the most. The output for this meeting is intended to give you enough information to produce a change management plan consisting of the activities to follow.

Vision and mission statements

Work with the project sponsor to articulate the vision and mission for your project.

THE WHY – Creating a vision statement

The vision statement should be a succinct, compelling statement outlining **why** your organisation is implementing the software, why this technology will deliver transformational value and how it helps you to deliver your overall business goals. Your vision verbalises the 'bigger picture' and conveys the direction the organisation is heading in.

How will the vision statement be used?

The vision statement should be used to articulate to the entire organisation, using your chosen medium, why we are undergoing this change and starting this project. It should be used as part of your change management strategy to gain buy-in to the concept. Having a vision provides aspirational direction for the organisation, encourages change acceptance, and enables an innovative mindset to consider 'the art of the possible' in what transformational value you can deliver once the technology is adopted.

What are best practice guidelines for a vision statement?

- Collaborate with the project sponsor and most senior head of change, transformation or IT roles.

- Obtain feedback from key stakeholders.

- Articulate why the technology helps us to achieve the future utopian vision for your organisation.

- Keep it to a short timeframe: I'd suggest no more than 18 months, to take into account changing technology or changes to your focus. (For example, consider how the pandemic resulted in so many businesses having to change their priorities and business plans.)

- Keep it clear, short and unambiguous.

- Make it unique to this software – articulate why this particular technology will contribute to the business achieving its stated goals.

- Ensure it is aligned to the overall business goals.

For example:

  - If the organisation has a goal to improve customer service, your vision should define how your software will deliver that.

  - If the organisation is focused on increasing profit or reducing costs, the technology you deliver should be enabling that.

  - If an organisational goal is improving staff retention and employee experience, the vision should define how it will save time, be easier to use or free up your people for more value-added activities.

THE WHAT – Creating a mission statement

The mission statement is a general statement of **what** you will do to achieve your vision. This describes the actions you will take to deliver that utopian vision to the business.

How will the mission statement be used?

The mission statement can also be used as part of your communication strategy to the whole organisation. But specifically, the mission statement needs to provide clarity and focus to the project team who are accountable for delivering the vision.

What are best practice guidelines for a mission statement?

- The mission statement should be more detailed and specific than your vision statement.
- The mission statement states what you are going to do within the timeframe specified in your vision.
- Keep it realistic, achievable and agreed with your sponsor.
- Ensure your mission statement is simple and easy to remember.
- Collaborate on creating this with your teams to ensure they are aligned and committed to the focus.

THE HOW – Creating the objectives

Objectives can be created later in the timeline when you know the necessary detail, but these are specific actions, expectations and timelines for how the project team will deliver the mission and vision.

How will objectives be used?

The objectives should be given to the team to define the critical deliverables and milestones required. Each objective should form the building blocks to deliver the actions you said you would do in your mission statement. They can be short term or long term.

What are best practice guidelines for objectives?

- Objectives should be written to be specific, measurable, achievable, relevant and timebound (SMART).
- Everyone in the team should have their own individual objectives or understand how the work they are doing contributes to the team objectives.
- These should be aligned with the corporate strategy and goals.
- They should be reviewed every quarter with the individual or team.

Responsible, accountable, consulted and informed (RACI matrix)

At this stage of the project, we only need a high-level RACI matrix, describing which roles should be responsible (does the work), accountable (ensure the work gets done), consulted (involved) and informed for the main activities. Include your project sponsor, project manager, comms manager and change manager when drafting this.

Later in the project you may want to consider a RACI with your Super Users, detailing the individual activities from your change plan, as a result of output from your change impact analysis or ADKAR surveys.

Organisational design

As to how extensive this will be depends on the change you are implementing. Are you upgrading a system version? If so, your existing employees will need to learn the new process or functionality and no other changes may be needed. But if you are implementing a new system or technology that requires new thinking and big changes in ways of working, you may need to rethink how your organisational structure should look to best align with your strategic vision and performance goals. Do you need to centralise departments? Do you need a location change or remote work to take advantage of available talent? Do you need to outsource any activity? Are you implementing a system that will require team upskilling or expanding: for example marketing database skills for a new customer relationship management system? Are you implementing a whole new technology such as intelligent automation that will require recruiting a new department, new skills and new roles? Do lines of reporting need to change?

The key is to think if you were starting from scratch today, with everything you know now, and the technology already in place, who would you need and where would you need them? Consult HR and your organisational design experts and be sure to be as transparent as you can with your workforce. Please do not rush into any redundancies or consultation; in my experience companies often underestimate how many people they will need after the software Go Live; your people will be slower on the system at first and you will need enough people in place to mitigate this as well as deliver your usual service levels.

Stakeholder analysis and mapping

We need a session with our project sponsor and project leads to identify the key stakeholders for our project. This will be a big brainstorm of who needs to be involved, who needs to be informed, whose departments are impacted and whose help we need. I would recommend just scribbling names on sticky notes and passing them to the facilitator to place on a whiteboard. We are going to place these names onto a power and influence grid (see Figure 8.1). This will give us a good output for both our comms plan and who we need to invite to a case for change session.

A personal recommendation for you though is to not just consider your project; that is, are there people in your organisation who have a lot of influence, are well thought of, highly networked – but otherwise may not have any involvement in or be affected by your project? These are still good people to include; keep them in your comms plan as they will inevitably have conversations with others in the organisation and we need them to report favourably on our project and goals.

Another thing to consider is where the stakeholders see themselves on the grid in Figure 8.1. I guarantee there will be one name you all think of who will want to be in that Manage closely bracket. You know the type I mean: the vocal ones, the ones who think of themselves as more important than they are, the ones who will sulk if not consulted. The x/y axis might not place them naturally in that grid space, but for the interests of politics and not wanting their negativity about your implementation, it may still be worth placing them in the grid where they want to be. I would also make sure you keep this output confidential as of course all your leaders have the ego to want to be seen as high power and influence. Just don't tell them I said that.

Figure 8.1 Power and influence stakeholder mapping grid

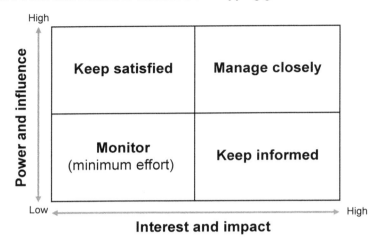

Case for change

A case for change session has many benefits: it encourages buy-in, gives you key insights as to what your next steps should be and helps you to demonstrate your utopian vision. A case for change session can take place virtually but may benefit from being face to face and could potentially be a full day session for a substantial change. Your stakeholders from the previous activity should be invited, as should your Super Users and representatives from the impacted departments. If Super Users have not been identified at this stage, look out for the ones who are enthusiastic about the change. They could be perfect people to recruit for it. Preferably do not invite all managers, we need team members too, but you might want to explain this to each head of department so they don't get upset at you for excluding them.

When thinking of your structure for the day, think about what information you most need. I would recommend the activities below.

- **Describe 'As-Is' process:**
  - Invite discussion on issues and disadvantages of the current system or ways of working.
- **Describe future 'To-Be' vision:**
  - Ideally have a senior executive or project sponsor to host this section.
  - Answer questions.
  - Invite discussion on whether any previously mentioned issues are resolved (let us hope so).
  - Have an activity to split into groups or breakout rooms to produce a two-minute 'elevator pitch' for the benefits of the new system or project and how it helps with the company goals. The elevator pitch involves producing a persuasive way

of describing the project in two minutes or less. Imagine you are in an elevator (well, I call it a lift as I'm British, but elevator pitch still just sounds better) and the CEO enters. How do you explain why we should do this project to the CEO? You may already have this locked down; if you do not then you will get ideas, but even if you do, getting key stakeholders to do this gets them committed to the outcome.

- **People:**

  o In groups or as a whole, invite contributions to capture how people will be impacted by this change and any necessary considerations.

- **Process:**

  o In groups or as a whole, invite contributions to capture how processes will be impacted by this change; that is, what ways of working will need to be redesigned?

- **Technology:**

  o In groups or as a whole, invite contributions to capture how technology will be impacted by this change such as reporting or system integrations that we need to plan for.

  o For these last three sections, you could use flipcharts or online whiteboards to capture what we need to be aware of.

- **Communications:**

  o Ask participants what they would suggest for a communications plan. What media or methods would they prefer, how often do they want to be communicated to and who by.

- **Training**

  o Announce the intended use of Super Users to help with training – introduce them if they are in the room. Use this opportunity to explain how important committing their time to the project will be. Ideally have your project sponsor there to reinforce this message. There may be managers in the room who have Super Users in their team already doing a day job; we need to ensure they are reassured that their roles will be temporarily backfilled, and that managers see the time away from their usual role as a development opportunity for the Super User, which will ultimately benefit their teams in the long run.

  o Ask participants to voice their preferred training methods. This will give you insights on whether they feel virtual or classroom training is adequate. Do people need upskilling on other digital skills? How much attention will departments need on this? How do they see Super Users being utilised?

  o Again, you may already have your own ideas on this, and of course you are the expert. I know you know best. But doing this sometimes gives you things you have not considered or reinforces that your original plan was the right one. But most importantly, by getting people involved in the learning design at this stage, they are then subconsciously invested in seeing the success of the project using their ideas.

Persona profiling

You will likely have personas and user journeys mapped out for how your new software is used. There will be similarities so it is worth consulting those. However, here we are talking about mapping the persona for those who are impacted by the change. This should be the key stakeholders we have identified and representatives from the areas you have identified as most impacted by the change. A persona should not be based on a real person, but a stereotype of the stakeholder or user in the particular area. The output of this is to consider how change will impact real people and plan how to best support them or empower them. Many actions could be added to your change plan because of considering this support.

Consider articulating and capturing:

- **Who**: Give them a fictional name and typical job title.

- **Profile**: Current workload, skill level and other factors (have they had a lot of change or new systems?).

- **Motivations**: How engaged are they with the organisation, how motivated or otherwise are they likely to be about the change or new system, what are their personal or role-based goals?

- **Empathy**: How are they likely to feel about the change and react?

Change impact analysis

In the initiation meeting we mapped a high-level list of who is impacted. Here we need to capture some detail. I would recommend using a spreadsheet and working with your project team and potentially some key stakeholders. Use the output to plan what you can do to support the change: if we want success, we cannot force this on people, we need to involve them and take them along with us through the change journey. Table 8.1 shows an example of a spreadsheet to capture change impact analysis.

You can also consider the scoring shown in Table 8.1, so we can see which department has the most impacted roles and the highest impact levels.

Table 8.1 Change impact analysis example

Who		What			Type of impact	How	
Department impacted	Roles impacted	What is the impact	As-Is	To-Be	Impact level L/M/H	People/ process/ technology etc.	What intervention is needed to support the change?	Comments
		Description						

Heatmap

Now we have determined the departments and roles impacted, we need to take a total organisation view. We need to involve project managers and HR and maybe other leaders for this activity. What other changes are being implemented in this timeframe? What other projects are they involved in? Are any other systems or training being planned at the same time? Are there any seasonal impacts to their workload? Consider the time involved for the roles and departments at each stage of your project: that is, during build, testing and training. Map this out on a quarterly or monthly basis (x axis) and indicate for each department what is happening to them and when (y axis). Where there is a lot of change happening at once for a particular group, use red or dark colours to indicate if multiple changes are happening in the same timeframe for a particular team. This will help you to visually identify teams that are facing a high volume of change and may need additional support (see Table 8.2). This output can affect your planned timeline (or preferably the other projects' timeline; let's make them move their project milestones instead). Joking aside, you need to take a priority view on what comes first and think about how humans react to too much change at once, as well as any impact on their workload.

Table 8.2 Heatmap example

	Month	January	February	March
Impacted team	Project activity			
HR	Project 1 Testing	X		
HR	Project 1 Training		X	
HR	Project 1 Go Live			X
HR	Project 2 Training	X		
HR	Project 2 Go Live		X	
HR	Project 2 Hypercare			X

Comms strategy

We now know our stakeholders and we know from our case for change how our teams want to receive communications, so we can use this to generate a strategy for each group of people, and our Super Users are a group here, too, remember. Use all the output so far to have a strategy planning meeting with your communications manager. We will cover suggestions for a comms plan in the next chapter but remember to have this meeting as we want to ensure your comms manager is not producing a generic plan, but tailoring it to the output of your hard work so far and ensuring Super Users play a part.

Change education

Here we are going to invite our Super Users, people managers and other optional key stakeholders to an educational session on managing change. The list below is a suggestion for the session:

- Provide introduction to change management principles.
- Discuss case studies of organisational change:
  - Brainstorm why organisational change initiatives may fail (lack of training, comms, leadership, etc.).
  - On average 70% of change projects fail in organisations.[2]
  - Are there any examples of good or bad changes from your own company?
  - Prompt a discussion on what we need to do to be in the 30% that succeed.
  - Consider a discussion using famous case studies of companies who failed to use digital transformation to stay relevant – for example, Betamax, Kodak, Blockbusters, Nokia. More recently, Skype. (How did Skype go from a word as synonymous with instant messaging and video calls, as Google is to searching, to then hardly being used during the Covid pandemic?)
  - **See Chapter 21 on project failure research for more information.**
- Present the change curve:
  - Where are they currently on the change curve? Where are their colleagues? (See Figure 8.2.)
- How does the brain handle change?
  - A different part of the brain handles all routine tasks and uses little energy, from the part of the brain that processes our response to change and uses a lot of energy. Our brain is designed to conserve energy, which is why we are hardwired to avoid change.

Figure 8.2 Change curve (Source: Shutterstock Photo ID: 1108804823, Licensed by Jayne Mather)

---

2   Nohria, N. and Beer, M. (2000) Cracking the code of change. *Harvard Business Review.* https://hbr.org/2000/05/cracking-the-code-of-change

- This theory from neuroscience should help organisations to understand how change resistance is part of being human, and can be draining and anxiety inducing if we force change on to people, rather than support them on the journey through to acceptance and engagement.

  ○ **See Chapter 18 for more detail on neuroscience.**

- Discuss how to spot and mitigate change resistance:

  ○ People who appear hesitant, disengaged or indifferent.

  ○ People who are expressing frustration.

  ○ People making negative comments about the implementation.

  ○ People avoiding using the system or attending training.

  ○ Discuss potential responses to change resistance:

    ▪ Ensure communication plans have relayed the vision, the benefits to the organisation as well as to the employees, the project plan and the training plan.

    ▪ Listen to people and provide opportunities for opinions to be discussed.

    ▪ Address any particular fears or concerns and debunk any myths.

    ▪ Be honest and transparent about any organisational design implications, while also offering a support structure for anyone affected.

    ▪ Request their input if they have expert advice or suggestions.

    ▪ Provide more information or FAQs.

    ▪ Host a software demonstration and Q&A.

    ▪ Provide more system training and practice sessions.

    ▪ Have senior management reinforce key messages.

    ▪ See the next section for more information on change resistance.

- Present output of change impact analysis:

  ○ Invite their ideas on supporting these changes.

- Introduce them to the Prosci® ADKAR Model (see p. 66):

  ○ Advise them on their role in ADKAR; that is, they will produce or manage an action plan for the area they look after on how they can mitigate any change resistance identified and improve the ADKAR scores.

Change resistance

Consider how you can combat what is causing change resistance in end users. Do not be dismissive of people's feelings. Just because you or your IT team may be excited for the new software does not mean all of your wider organisation will be. We need to solicit how people are feeling following any announcements. Use your Super Users as conduits to obtain insight into how end users are feeling. What are people's perceptions, fears or objections?

- Is it pain from a previous project that did not go well? Be honest about how that happened and communicate the lessons learned or how we will do things differently.

- Are people worried emerging technology will replace jobs? Be transparent: will job descriptions change or will people be moved into other departments? Will we retrain and provide new skills to people? Will we free up some of their time to enable them to do more value-added or intellectually stimulating activities? Be honest, but also consider how we can counteract this fear by winning hearts and minds.

- Are people experts on the current system and do not want to have to start again? Mine these people for process information or user requirements. Maybe you or the Super Users feel the same and we can create solidarity by learning the new system together.

- Are there people with significant expertise who feel they are not being consulted? There are occasions when leaders make the wrong decisions or project managers select the wrong software. If you have subject matter experts who can attest and articulate why they feel the change is the wrong one for the organisation then ensure they are consulted – they may have insights you have not considered.

- Speak to people, or more importantly, listen. Involve your communication leads and sponsors in planning how we can reduce or manage this resistance. Use your Super Users as change agents here to talk to people, to feed back to you and to strategically convey reassuring messages in response.

- **See Chapter 17 and the Eleven Step Super User Change Model for more information on this.**

Prosci ADKAR® Model

There are other measurements you can use to determine how ready your people and organisation are to accept the change and the new system, but this is the one I would recommend from my experience with system projects. You will need to have a closer look at the ADKAR model, and there are survey tools that you will need to have a licence to use. It is well worth it as then your organisation can use this in the future for other projects.

We are going to survey all our people in the impacted departments at certain points in the project. We can combine surveys to send together if needed; it does not have to be done at different times. After each survey result, we will meet with our Super Users and change management team to analyse how high the scores are for each area and for individuals, and discuss why there may be differences between people in a department or between departments. Then we will create an action plan for how we can improve our scores. We can potentially then re-survey the same people – but certainly do not do that too soon; allow some time for any actions to have the intended effect, and you can potentially re-ask some questions with your next round of surveys.

Awareness: This survey should be conducted after the initial comms campaign. There is a list of questions you can choose for your survey, and you need to decide which is the most relevant. Recipients mark themselves as 1–5 on how aware they are of their role to play, their awareness of why the change is happening, how it contributes to our goals and if they know what the training or rollout plans are. When we get the results, we will know how effective our communications have been so far, and what actions we need to take to improve awareness. Maybe more leaders are needed to be involved with delivering the comms: are comms expected to be cascaded but this is not happening? Do we need to change our channels or frequency in our comms plan in any way?

Desire: I would recommend doing this after comms and after the case for change session. This will give us an indication of how willing, supportive and enthusiastic people are for the new system: are they convinced by the 'why', are they looking forward to the benefits, do they feel it will have a positive impact on them, their role or department? The resulting action plan does not always need to be a formal intervention; it could involve the Super User having conversations in the canteen, online check-ins or stopping by at their desks. It could be something more deliberate such as presenting a demonstration to the particular team to alleviate any concerns or hosting a Q&A session with them.

Knowledge: We would survey users after their systems training. Do they know what is expected of them in ways of working? Do they have the knowledge on how the system will work? Do they feel capable of using the system at Go Live? There are many other questions to choose from in the ADKAR tool and you can also make your own. These survey results may need a more comprehensive action plan. Are more training aids needed? Are more sessions needed? Has the training gone into enough detail? We know the training stage is often right before Go Live, so you may need to deal with actions by providing more support or use on-the-job training afterwards, but ADKAR is just a great tool to know this and to plan for it in advance.

Ability: I would recommend doing this survey shortly after Go Live when they are using the system for real. Do they have the ability to do their job? Do they know how to get the data they need from the system? Do they know where to go for additional knowledge, training and support? Do they feel capable? Do they feel they have knowledge gaps? Super Users can be so valuable in improving people's scores here: we can give more workshops, more coaching, get managers involved in setting behavioural expectations or run masterclasses to give a deeper dive on a particular subject.

Reinforcement: Here we would survey all project team members, stakeholders and end users, asking them: Is the organisation committed to sustaining this change? Are leaders encouraging successful adoption of the system? Do I see the benefits we were expecting? Do I have an outlet for providing feedback and improvement ideas? Is my performance on the new system or processes being evaluated and rewarded?

Whenever we do this work, we have to always ask ourselves – **So what?** Whether it is ADKAR or training course surveys, those results should always be the beginning of an evaluation. We have seen it many times that companies and training providers think that just sending a survey is the evaluation and then they're done; but no, we need to use the qualitative and quantitative data we obtain to make improvements and deliver more interventions. We need to use ADKAR to monitor low scoring areas and take action to improve them. We can measure change resistance through these scores, and can then plan what intervention is needed, scoring the effort required to improve and the risk if we don't – to provide the impetus as to why it is important to take further action. Remember that change curve: individuals and teams will go on a journey along it, the more we do to aid that progression, the more we are likely to see the benefits from a successful product adoption.

Training plan

Here we can move into our training planning stage, using the outputs from our case for change. We will cover this in a later chapter, but please do involve key stakeholders as well as Super Users in reviewing and approving your plan.

Business readiness

This could be done by your change team or your project manager, but Super Users need to have a voice in these meetings. These take place regularly towards the end of your project and are essentially a tool to decide a Go or No-Go decision for our planned Go Live date. Your sponsor needs to have the confidence to delay a Go Live if the criteria indicate you are not ready. If you Go Live just because of a date on a plan and not because the organisation is ready (I know there's budget and costs involved in extending) it will do more harm to your business, and potentially to your reputation with customers if we deploy without the right enablers in place. Push for the original date by all means, offer overtime and incentives, think of alternatives and mitigations, have crisis meetings to see what actions can be taken to try to meet the readiness criteria – but if this cannot be achieved, then a decision to delay will be more respected than a decision to deploy regardless.

You will need to decide your own criteria, but we would recommend using a RAG status (red, amber, green) to rate the following:

- *number of people trained;
- *number of critical roles trained (the people you cannot do without);
- attendance and absenteeism on training sessions (to calculate critical path analysis on how long to complete);
- standard operating procedures (SOPs) and training support published;
- ADKAR actions implemented;
- comms plan executed;
- *environment or system ready;
- *defects resolved (break down into risk status of defects: are they critical, nice to have, aesthetic);
- *user access, roles, permissions in place;
- *IT support model and hypercare support plan in place;

- operational readiness factors prepared – such as stock build for example or a reduction in backlog work or a freeze on material data changes;

- *cutover plan on track;

- rollout plan (phased, pilot or big bang Go Live) agreed that minimises operational disruption;

- Super User Go Live support plan in place;

- there may be other criteria relevant to your system and organisation.

*A red status here would indicate a No-Go decision.

Lessons learned and feedback

Plan this for three weeks after Go Live, and again at three months. This is particularly important if you are having a phased rollout so you can use this feedback to make changes before your next rollout milestone. We would recommend just a focus group, containing a selection of stakeholders, Super Users and end users. You want to ask for anecdotal comments, but also prompt the usual questions for this space – What did we do well? What could we do better? But consider specific questions too: 'Are managers and leaders supporting the change?' is a really important one in my experience.

To give you an example, I implemented a marketing leads system for field sales teams. Several salespeople were not using the system adequately to report the status of their converted leads and sales pipeline opportunities. I was asked by the leadership team to do more training with these teams. I could have just done this, ticked a box and walked away with a thank you from the leaders, but I wanted to find out why they were not updating their leads and bids on the system, so I asked them…

'I was using the system for my pipeline at first Jayne, but every week my manager was still asking me to write them in a spreadsheet to email to him, the same way we used to do it. It was too much work entering it on the system and on the spreadsheet. What is the point of doing both?'

It was not the sales teams that needed more training, it was the managers. They were not driving the right behaviours and they were not using the system dashboards we trained them on to get the information they needed. I quite enjoyed reporting that back to the leadership team. And I had to do that: we need the leaders to drive the managers. Change and system adoption has to be reinforced with the 'why'. And this is 'why' asking for this feedback is so important.

Benefits realisation

You need to be tracking this against the metrics that were written in the original business case. But this needs to be long-term thinking: for example, you will not see evidence of time saved until the system is fully embedded as people will be slow at first using a new system or process. Track benefits for at least 12 months: costs saved, hours saved, production rates, leads converted and so on. And again, we need to ask why, and implement a change plan if we are not seeing the results we expected. Is it more training, is it adoption, is it process improvement? If we are not tracking it, we cannot fix it.

Continuous improvement (CI)

Your Super Users need to be empowered to do what they think is right and needed at this stage. Does a way of working need changing, do we need to plan for a system enhancement, do we need workshops to enable or improve collaboration between departments? Your Super Users will know this, and this needs to be an agenda point in every Super User community call we do after Go Live.

It is crucial for leadership to provide support and encouragement, such as effective planning and prioritisation of proposed CI initiatives, a mechanism for requesting system changes or development, and an agreement to allow Super Users dedicated time for these activities even after the project is completed. A Super User is for life, not for Go Live.

Like with Super Users, we can see how the use of change management techniques needs to be threaded through the project from initiation to long after Go Live. It still doesn't guarantee success, but by doing the right things, it is much more likely.

Further learning

For more on organisational change management, and to see the dedicated change model for Super User networks (the Eleven Step Model) see Chapter 17.

9   HOW DO WE DEVELOP A COMMUNICATION PLAN?

Recommendations for creating a communications plan for your software project utilising a Super User network.

We are going to rely on our comms experts for this. You will have system development experts, change experts, leadership experts and, of course, your Super Users are the experts we create. We use the strengths of the people we have. This book is not to tell you how to be experts in everything for your software project, but it is about how we can use the expertise of our Super Users to aid each part of the plan. This is the same as with comms; the internal communications experts should use their knowledge and experience to create a comprehensive plan, but we need them to include our Super User specific recommendations.

The comms plan is likely to be one using the **AIDA** (awareness, interest, desire, action) **Model**, and should have aims such as:

- Generate **awareness** of the system, the change and the project.

- Create **interest** in learning more and receiving more comms.

- Ensure people have a **desire** for the change and understand how it benefits them.

- Provide a call to **action** to ensure people are engaged with the change and what they need to do.

If you have the budget, consider an outside agency who do this day in day out, creating innovative and effective campaigns. Get them creating great graphics, logos, slogans, animations and interactions about your project to generate some buzz. Whether external or internal comms, ask to be consulted on their ideas; you want to ensure the comms materials and your training materials have a consistent look and feel, preferably with a brand and name for your project.

We want to ensure Super Users are considered in the comms plan, and certainly that Super User Leads are heavily involved in the strategy and creation of the plan.

Here are the things I want you to consider in a comms plan:

To:	From:
Leaders and people managers	Project sponsor and CEO or CIO

We need to ensure the senior leadership team and people managers are briefed by the project sponsor on the importance of committing to using a Super User network.

The message needs to come from the top to stipulate:

- how key this role is;
- the support and time a Super User needs to give to the project;
- the recruitment criteria and campaign (see Chapter 5);
- the importance of backfilling roles (so that Super Users don't get pulled back into their previous duties during critical times for the project);
- the responsibilities Super Users will have;
- the impact Super Users will have;
- any line manager reporting changes;
- most importantly, the support and time that managers need to give to a Super User should a request be made from them.

To:	From:
Super Users	Comms manager, project sponsor or CEO

I have mentioned in their onboarding how important that welcome from a senior leader is, but it is not just important at the beginning. If your comms manager regularly meets with your sponsor or CEO, use that opportunity to get some quotes or a short video from them to continue thanking the Super Users for their contribution effort and dedication, especially if they can include detail on specific issues they've worked on. I cannot state enough how motivational it will be to the Super Users to know that the extra work they are doing is being noticed, and then we can get them to carry on doing more extra work, right? Don't worry, our Super Users will do that anyway if we follow all the tips in this book. Your Super Users will have forged close links with other workstreams, so they may have a good awareness of other activities, but these still need to be included in regular comms. Make sure your project manager is keeping the Super Users informed of project updates from the wider team.

To:	From:
Project manager and Super User Leads	Super Users

Your Super User Lead needs to establish reporting from your Super Users to get to the right people. Have them report back on a weekly or monthly basis, on some of the points listed below, with potentially lots more depending on the stage and scope of your project:

- ABC updates:
  - **A**ctivities, **b**enefits (value they have added) and **c**hallenges (blockers, concerns).
- Metrics:
  - Report on progress for specific activities: training attendance, course content written, SOPs written, defect status, % of cutover actions completed and any critical path analysis to confirm time to completion.

To:	From:
Key stakeholders, project manager, project sponsor, workstream leads, business process owners, line managers of Super Users	**Super User Lead**

Your comms manager needs to plan and schedule these comms updates from the Super User Lead to keep everyone updated on the Super User activity and to give it the attention and prominence it deserves. No particular recommendations on a channel – emails; regular slots in comms meetings; project updates – would all work.

We need this content to go to the project sponsor, to the project manager and any workstream leads or business process owners. It should be a high-level update consisting of:

- **Key metrics:** Reported from Super Users as mentioned previously such as testing hours, number of defects assigned, training courses written or delivered and so on.
- **Escalation:** If the critical path analysis of any activities indicates we may not complete all testing or training or defect resolution by the required milestone, then escalate it here for help with extra resource or crisis management.
- **Super User activities:** Their focus for the particular time period.
- **Super User recognition:** Call out the wins and their extra efforts.
- **Issue resolution:** The business process decisions made, defects resolved, end user tickets resolved and so on.

To:	From:
All end users and all colleagues	**Comms manager or team**

We know a lot is likely to be in their plan anyway for all end users of the system, and for all colleagues, but we need to make sure these aspects are mentioned in those comms:

- **Introduction to Super Users:** Who they are, what they will do and how key they are to the project's success. You could have Super User interviews or 20 Questions, for example – have a deeper insight into a different Super User each time.
- **Project updates:** What the project team and what the Super Users are currently working on.
- **Training details:** How much training will be delivered, what training methods we are using, when invites will go out, where training will take place, what parts are mandatory or optional, and any details such as if food is included if it is an after-hours or lunchtime session (it better be).
- **A countdown to Go Live**: Building excitement and reminding people of the vision and benefits.

- **The Go Live details**: Who will be where, how they will contact or identify their Super Users, and include the issue escalation support model from Chapter 4.
- **Communicate the wins:** The benefits after Go Live, Super User thanks and recognition or issues resolved.

To:	From:
All end users	Super Users

This could be just an email or included in other comms vehicles, but if you're likely to have regular content, consider a dedicated branded newsletter or magazine from your Super Users, with production support from your comms manager. A good idea I have used is to have each edition written and curated by a different Super User, or there may be an enthusiastic Super User who wants to lead on this. Include content such as:

- **Super User column:** Highlight a different Super User in each newsletter to give readers a chance to learn more about the people who are making a difference. Ask the Super User to share their thoughts and experiences.
- **Transparency:** Address anything you feel is not working well, what issues/fixes are in progress, what would Super Users like to improve on in the future, what enhancement ideas have they submitted.
- **Best practice:** What process tips and advice would a Super User give to an end user.
- **System tip of the month or week:** We can expand here on what we could not cover in training: what will make things quicker for end users, what data can we extract or report on, what advanced training did the Super User receive that we can now start to pass on in a drip feed fashion.
- **Coming soon:** Include what training refreshers or workshops are scheduled, what is going to be featured in the next software upgrade, what development or enhancement has been tested and due to be deployed.
- **FAQs:** What questions are Super Users being asked the most: include the answers here to get the information more widely known.
- **Other ideas:** I guarantee you, an engaged Super User community will have lots more ideas of what to include in such a newsletter or magazine.

Try to keep this going for as long as possible, not just for hypercare. If you start to struggle for content, reduce the frequency as you go along from weekly, to monthly, to quarterly and potentially, but not preferred, biannually.

10   HOW DO WE DEVELOP A TRAINING PLAN?

The methods, options and recommendations for creating an end user training plan that will drive adoption of your new system.

Hold your breath: this chapter is going to be a long one. Why? Arguably it is the most important. Take notes here and be prepared to prove that there is no such thing as just trainers. Your L&D or education team are made up of data analysts, instructional designers, consultants, facilitators, adult learning experts, curriculum developers, learning & development advisers, business partners, software tutors and more, and often, all in the same person.

A training plan should be formally written, and approved by your stakeholders, to capture all the activities you are planning. We want to do this so that senior executives understand that training involves more than just the delivery of a webinar. By getting your full plan signed off, they are committing to best practices that are required to achieve the ultimate goal – adoption of your new software.

PREPARATION FOR A TRAINING PLAN

Learning needs analysis (LNA)

Before we build any training or decide what the training looks like, we need to know who we are training, what they currently know and what they need to know. That is because learning professionals never default to just producing a requested elearning course or delivering a classroom course to impart information; they only do that if the analysis determines that to be the right approach. It might be that an online walkthrough of new features will suffice, or a PDF quick reference guide, or it might be several weeks of workshops; we need to do our analysis first to propose the solution that will best meet the company objectives – the 'why' of why we're introducing new technology.

This should be a collaborative exercise with your project sponsor for the vision, your business leads for the processes, the technical leads who understand the software, and line managers or Super Users who understand the audience.

A spreadsheet is a good output, and I would recommend incorporating the headings listed below, adapted to suit.

- **Audience:**
  - Who are your learners (external suppliers, external customers, internal departments, internal roles)?

- Do not forget to include your Super Users as a separate audience group, as by definition they will need any training at a higher competency level.

An example from my experience. A new product creation process on a new material management system meant:

- education for external suppliers to input additional material data directly onto our new online system;
- education for warehouse teams for receiving and storing the item;
- education for procurement to purchase the item using the system;
- education for the supply chain for forecasting, demand and supply planning;
- education for the new product introduction teams on collating information and setting up the product;
- education for the web and marketing team for extracting source data for their content.

The same system, the same scenario of a new product, meant each of these groups needed educating in a different way, to differing expertise levels with different objectives.

- **Use case:**
  - List the scenarios or tasks that the new software will be used for.
  - Use your spreadsheet as a matrix to capture which audience groups need to be educated on which use case.
- **Method of execution:**
  - How will they perform the process?
    - Brief overview of what the task entails; ways of working; system information and screens/transactions used.
    - It may be helpful for the future to cross-reference this with the names of any process flows or existing documentation.
- **Objectives:**
  - What will be the positive impact or benefit of knowing how to successfully perform this task?
    - Capture metrics if they exist yet.
    - Capture who the benefit is for (customer, organisation, department).
- **Competency level:**
  - To what level of understanding do they need to know how to do this task?
  - Consider **the Three E's of Competency:**

- Do they need an overview of the process? (**Essential**)
- Do they need to learn basic functionality? (**Efficiency**)
- Do they need to become experts in the full system capability? (**Excellence**)
    - Establishing this will guide us to tailor the training to the specific needs of the users.
- **As-Is or To-Be changes:**
    - Does the audience already know the process or the system?
    - How big a change is it from what they used to do?
- **Behaviours (desired and undesired):**
    - Regardless of the system, do we need our learners to behave in a new way? Are we using the new process or technology to influence ways of working?
        - An example using the system we just mentioned: a desired behaviour may be to check vendor input to the system to ensure product information is right first time before passing it to the planning or purchasing stage. An undesired behaviour may be discontinuing a material without informing the marketing team to update web content first or stopping the practice of only sporadically checking for new material requests.
        - By identifying and promoting desired behaviours and addressing undesired behaviours, organisations can ensure that the new system or process can be used to promote positive optimised ways of working.
- **Accountability:**
    - Who is ultimately responsible for ensuring the process or software is used correctly to deliver the objectives described?
        - Note: it should be the managers, not us.
- **Knowledge and ability:**
    - current knowledge of process or technology;
    - current ability level in using the software.
- **Skill gaps:**
    - What skills do the workforce need before they can use the software?

For example, before teaching developers how to use new artificial intelligence (AI) software, it was essential to ensure that they had a solid foundation in AI fundamentals, industry trends, use cases, concepts and the theory of how AI works.

In another project, some of the warehouse team needed PC literacy before I could show them their new SAP software system for goods receiving.

Before I trained salespeople how to use a new online customer relationship management app, we needed to teach them how to use their iPads first. When

I said, 'tap on this icon to open the app', voices came from the back of the room to ask me to show them how to turn on and set up their iPad first. Because of assumptions, I had not planned that as part of the training, so it took much longer. Then there was the time when I said to take a screenshot and some took out their mobile phones to take a picture of the iPad screen. It makes me laugh now, but the fault was not with the learner, but with me for not doing the right analysis up front.

- **Training proposal:**
  - What are your initial thoughts on how you can best get the audience to learn how to do the task described and bridge any skill gaps?
  - You would only complete this column after having gathered all the information you need.

Training proposal

Take into account the outputs from your case for change where we asked those impacted how they would best learn the content (see Chapter 8) and from your LNA, and produce a high-level overview to share with your stakeholders on what the training approach will look like. We should have already had buy-in before this stage for Super Users but do still mention this group here as well as your end users. This may be a plan on a page, or a PowerPoint™ presentation.

Note: L&D need to advise the business of the suggested solution; they do not take a directive to just deliver a course, or build an elearning course. They are not order-takers, they act here in the role of professional consultants or business partners and advise the best training solution (from many options listed later in this chapter) to achieve the project aims.

Training approach meeting

We should then hold a meeting with the sponsor, project manager and other key stakeholders. Here you would present your proposal to gain verbal agreement to your plans, being prepared to consider any of their suggestions. The output from this meeting will contribute to your full formal training plan.

Content mapping

Use your LNA outputs on what tasks need to be trained and do an exercise to map tasks against what supporting content you need. This might be existing content you can repurpose or recreate, or it might be graphics, presentations, videos or other media that need creating. For each task on your content map ensure you capture any key messaging or narrative that needs to be included, links to existing content as well as details of other collateral needed to cover the topic. This is useful to be given to your instructional designers to help with any content creation.

Design specifications

If you have decided on elearning, or other content to be produced in-house or by a third-party provider, you will need to create a design specification detailing exactly what they need to create. This should include:

- purpose of content creation;
- course name;
- course description;
- course objectives;
- number of modules and titles;
- module structure and expected topics and content;
- style, design and branding details;
- type of content (infographic, immersive elearning, ebook, etc.);
- target audience;
- skill level;
- expected length, size and duration;
- outputs from content mapping;
- contact details for project owner and SME;
- expected timescales.

CREATING A TRAINING PLAN

Now we have completed the exercises to know what we want to create, and we have done the office politics thing of involving our senior stakeholders to get their buy-in and wisdom in the training approach meeting, we are going to hold them to their commitments and write out a formal training plan with written approval.

This puts everything you want to do in the project plan, and ensures that, for example, they understand that after Go Live, evaluation work will continue with potentially further training interventions, and they will understand the importance of comprehensive Super User upskilling.

Training plan contents

Your plan needs to include aspects from all steps in the **ADDIE** (analysis, design, development, implementation, evaluation) Model.

- **Analysis:**
  - What analysis has been done, or requires doing?

- **Design:**
  - What will be the look and feel of your training?
  - What media or methods will you use?
- **Development:**
  - What content or material is required? How long will it take to create?
- **Implementation:**
  - How will training be delivered, reported and managed?
- **Evaluation:**
  - How will you measure the success of the training against both the project vision and course objectives?
  - What action will you take if the evaluation indicates we are not meeting the success criteria?

You know your project best, so adapt the following suggestions to suit your plan, but building on the concept above I would recommend the headings below in your training plan.

Introduction

Keep this brief. The people who are reading the document will know what the project is about, and why we are implementing the new technology. But describe in a couple of sentences or less why the training plan has been written, any background as to why the change is happening or why the training is needed, and any information on what is or is not in scope for the training.

Executive summary

If your sponsor, CEO or most senior stakeholder does not read all of your 16 pages, what key things do you want them to know? Like your elevator pitch I mentioned in the change chapters, we need to articulate and justify in a concise way why our plan determines we need a mandatory elearning course or just PDF on-the-job training aids, or eight weeks of workshops to cover all the content.

Points of contact

This needs to be a list of names of whomever you want to read the document, sign it or help you at some point along the way.

Approvers:

- project sponsor;
- project manager;

- product owner;
- IT lead (especially if you have requirements for test environments, equipment, etc.).

Contributors:

- communications lead;
- change management lead;
- business process owner or lead;
- Super User Lead (if not the author).

Reviewers:

- key stakeholders;
- heads of departments impacted;
- instructional designers.

Document organisation

Provide links to any other documents or folders that are mentioned or pertinent to the project, such as:

- change management documents;
- communications plan;
- content library or content map;
- design specifications;
- learning needs analysis;
- process documentation;
- project documentation;
- training session plans.

Change management outputs

If there were any key outputs from the change management activities, such as your case for change or initial ADKAR surveys, then highlight them here to justify the choices you have made. Or at least mention what change management activities have taken place. The change management and L&D teams should remain closely aligned along the way.

Learning needs analysis outputs

Highlight what collaborative work was completed in the LNA from the beginning of this chapter and how this supported your decisions.

Design and approach agreed

Give a brief overview of the outputs from your training approach meeting, to describe what they have committed to; include any details of project branding if relevant.

Communications plan

Obviously, we are not going to include the full comms plan here. That is a separate document to be approved – but do highlight what you have agreed for comms about training sessions, awareness or advertising pieces, Super User newsletters and so on.

Super User training programme

Detail what the curriculum will look like for the Super Users. Add key milestones and dates, any dependencies, how many sessions for them to receive their training, how many weeks planned for system familiarisation, how many days to practice session delivery, how many training sessions they will each deliver and any other necessary details. Present this in a formal, structured way so they can see the exact requirements needed to enable both Super User upskilling, and to deliver what the end users need.

End user training curriculum

Describe what options you have chosen to make up your end user training curriculum. Below is not an exhaustive list but ideas to consider.

- **Training documents**:
  - standard operating procedure (SOP);
  - infographic;
  - quick reference guide;
  - user guide or system operating manual;
  - ebook;
  - poster;
  - job aid;
  - flash cards;
  - workbook;
  - presentation slide deck;
  - exercise or assessment;
  - technical help documentation;
  - installation guide.
- **Training media:**
  - demo video;

- teaser or preview video;
- CEO or sponsor video;
- 'How-To' video tutorial;
- podcast.

- **Training methodology**:
  - blended (recommended);
  - elearning;
  - webinars;
  - classroom session (Are they passive demos or interactive with practice?);
  - drop-in session for optional system practice (either a dedicated room or online labs);
  - exams or certification;
  - on-the-job instruction or tutorials;
  - social learning groups;
  - executive or senior leadership sessions;
  - digital mentors (or reverse mentoring).

- **Digital support**:
  - digital adoption platforms:
    - step-by-step wizards
    - product tours
    - online process walkthroughs
    - tool tip help
    - embedded 'How-To' videos
  - online help portal for end users;
  - knowledge base;
  - a test or training system with prebuilt exercises;
  - dedicated intranet space.

- **Merchandise**:
  - mouse mats, notebooks and so on, with system tips or instructions on them;
  - Super User identification (hats, badges, clothes);
  - branded stationery for end users attending training.

Development timeline

Document the time required to produce drafts and storyboards, gain approval from stakeholders, and create the final materials and media.

Training administration

Document what needs to happen to facilitate the training being delivered:

- Physical location or virtual environment (e.g. webinar tool, Zoom or Teams).
- Number of rooms/sessions required and capacity.
- Schedules and dates.
- How many sessions or subjects does each audience group have to attend?
- Resource planning (how many from a department can be trained at once, shift schedules, absence and holiday planning).
- Administration: Who will send invites, print handouts and prepare room.
- How the attendance will be recorded and reported.
- If training or elearning is mandatory or optional and who will report completion rate.
- Completion criteria: Just attend or watch, or must they pass an exam or competency assessment?

Course objectives or learning outcomes

List what the objectives will be for each course. This might be objectives for each audience type, such as we captured in our LNA. Or it might be per course, but we need to use our LNA again here to understand to what competency level (the Three E's of Competency) each group needs to learn a particular topic to.

When writing your objectives, start with 'By the end of this course you will be able to...'. And then we need our verbs to follow this. It could be 'recognise, describe, summarise, or explain' for a basic competency level. It could be 'demonstrate, apply, perform, run, analyse, execute' for a more comprehensive understanding. Research Bloom's Taxonomy verbs for help when writing your course objectives.

Writing objectives is a skill that needs practising. It took me a long time in the beginning to stop writing 'understand' for everything. But that is too broad; the taxonomy above really helps but another tactic is to consider what a user will be able to do, consistently, in six months' time if your training was successful. Critique your objectives by checking if what you have articulated is something we can measure, observe or assess and are we transferring knowledge or are we facilitating performance-related actions?

Training storage

Document where end users will go for training support. Is it the learning management system (LMS), a portal or a SharePoint page for example. Consider ease of use here too. I know you love your LMS and want to get value out of it, and it is ideal for initial training so we get the pass and completion rate reporting. But is it quick enough for users to access what they need, when they need it? For more on knowledge management techniques, see Chapter 20.

Consider if they can pin courses in the LMS, or create collections or favourites so they can get back to them quickly. Or is it a longer process to log in, search for what they need, enrol and then launch a course? Would they have to sit through or fast forward a 20-minute video just to get to the part they need? Would it be quicker for them to just favourite the SharePoint links for a quick reference guide or micro-learning video so they can get to what they need quickly at the point of use? This is why you might want to consider digital adoption platforms, so your training support is embedded in the product interface to access at the point of use.

Previous content

Document whose responsibility it is to archive, delete or update any existing content with previous ways of working.

Evaluation

We will look at your options for this in a coming chapter. But list your plans here for how you will evaluate your training, the milestone dates for reporting and affirm your commitment to potentially deliver further training, or change management activities, should the evaluation results determine it is needed to increase adoption of the technology and to deliver the benefits described.

Business readiness

If the proposal for this is fully documented in your change management plan, there is no need to repeat it here. If it's not, do include it (see recommendations in Chapter 8) or perhaps just mention the criteria relating to training that you will report on: for example the number of users we need to ensure are trained before we say we are ready to Go Live.

Rollout plan

Your project manager should take care of this with you, but they cannot do it without Super User contribution and commitment. Your implementation plan needs to document how you are going live:

- Is it a phased rollout – region by region, department by department?
- Is it a big bang with the whole end user population going live at once?

- Will the legacy system be switched off or run in parallel?
- Is it a pilot group? Proof of concept?
- Is it a minimum viable product (MVP) aimed at a limited amount of users or with limited features? How will the rollout plan differ when the software transitions from MVP to fully released software?
- Are the intended users in one location? One organisation? One department?
- Where will the Super Users be? Where will the project team be?

You need to consider if you have adequate IT support and Super User resource to manage whichever option: are they going to be available remotely or on site? How will you manage this geographically? This plan needs to cover all these aspects on a week-by-week basis.

Hypercare

Although it may not be your decision how long the hypercare period will last after Go Live, record in your training plan what role your Super Users will play. Are they 'boots on the ground'? If so, does this require travel and accommodation? Are they just floor walking to support end users? Are they involved in the investigation, testing and diagnosis of any defects? Are they delivering any further training sessions?

Business as usual (BAU) procedures

Your IT team will determine your support model, but it could be your or internal comms responsibility to ensure this is presented in a user-friendly way (see Chapter 4 Stage 4 for an example). Essentially you want to ensure an end user reports any issues to the Super User first, as they did in hypercare, as well as check in a knowledge base if you have one, before any IT ticket is raised.

I have already called out how a Super User is expected to cascade best practice techniques and further training on an ongoing basis. Similarly, we want to ensure it is expected that Super Users are empowered to explore future continuous improvement – we want them to have quarterly workshops to maybe suggest software enhancements, process changes or problem-solving activities. Use this section to state they are to be given the time, the responsibility and potentially the training to make this happen.

Future training

Ensure it is documented how training will be conducted in the future, once you are in BAU.

- **New colleagues**:
  - Do Super Users train them one on one? Is elearning automatically assigned to their roles? Do they learn on the job with training materials?
  - Work with HR to ensure systems training is covered in an onboarding programme.

- This should be the case for all the systems they need, not just our new one.

- **Change control**:
  - How will materials be updated if the system or processes are changed?
  - Will it be a Super User or L&D responsibility to own training materials?

- **Refreshers**:
  - Document that Super Users will be required to attend Super User calls to maintain their knowledge levels.
  - Super Users will then be required to cascade best practice information to end users from these sessions as well as provide regular refresher training on key processes.
  - A mechanism should be designed to record that best practice and refresher training is actually cascaded to the end user teams.
    - Our Super Users are of course brilliant, but we need to hold them accountable for doing this. It should be in their objectives, so evidence is recorded of them doing this.

Super User succession planning

This is so important you need to call it out in its own section. We must ensure we continue to have Super Users to support the system for as long as it exists, so as people inevitably leave or change roles, the manager should nominate new Super Users to take their place. You may need fewer Super Users years down the line, but we still need to maintain those best practice standards and ensure continuous improvement is delivered, instigated by this group. Consider how you will maintain this coverage.

In Chapter 15 we will look at assessing our user maturity. You can use this to identify potential candidates for future Super Users.

Issues and recommendations

You were already a talented professional, and now you are reading this book you have even more power to influence a successful transformative project. However, it is ultimately the responsibility of line managers and department heads to ensure that people use the software in the correct ways and drive the correct behaviours. State this explicitly in this section.

There may be other things that you have not been able to secure, things that you want but have not been given. Perhaps IT have not committed to giving you a test or training environment to enable users to practise on; perhaps you have not been given the room or equipment you needed to set up a drop-in practice room. Maybe there is a particular authoring tool, or screen recording tool that would accelerate the production of training materials. Get it in writing here. It might not change anything, but write down what you need to improve the chances of success.

Approval

Finally, you need a section to request that your signatories have read, agreed and commit to supporting your plan.

Further learning:

For more on Super User upskilling, see Chapter 11.

For a complete suggested session plan for a train the trainer course, see Chapter 12.

For more on delivering and designing software training, see Chapters 13 and 14.

For a suggested evaluation and adoption strategy, see Chapter 15.

11 HOW DO WE DEVELOP A SUPER USER EDUCATION PROGRAMME?

A detailed curriculum for upskilling and educating your Super Users.

What does the Super User need to know to be effective at the role, and how will they be supported? Upskilling should be occurring throughout the project: this is another reason why we believe Super Users should be recruited at the beginning and not just for the training stage. This chapter describes the interventions that I believe should form part of the Super User development plan.

Onboarding

In Chapter 7 we discussed an onboarding session for your Super Users. Soon after recruitment you need a large welcome event to set the scene for what the Super User role consists of, and to start your journey of having a collaborative community. Follow this event by adding the Super User to any groups, chats or social media you have. This ensures they are starting the experience with all the relevant information.

Project team

Next, I suggest you include time with your project team for each Super User. It may be that Super Users are split into different business processes, or they will concentrate on several processes for their own area. They need to know the structure of the project team and who will be involved in each process. Introduce them to the key roles that they will work with. This is better done in person to build a relationship but can be done virtually or by distributing the information. The project sponsor should have also been introduced at the onboarding stage, with a thank you and a welcome.

Project plan

Schedule some time for the Super Users with your project manager. This could be done virtually depending on the number of Super Users you have and their geographical location. Ensure the project manager walks them through the aim of the project, the strategic milestones and then goes into detail about the project plan. With the project manager, use this time to elaborate more on what role the Super User will play at each stage of the project using the information in this book. Make sure the project manager is open to tweaking the project plan to reflect any recommendations from the Super Users, based on their expertise. Remember to make sure the plan has a defect resolution or retesting stage before training delivery. If not, call it out. We don't want the training window to be squeezed by this not being planned for.

Change management

We might be implementing a system into an organisation, but what we are really doing is inflicting change onto a group of people. You will have seen it yourselves: there will be the ones who are excited about the change and wanting to be involved, the ones who remain passive and indifferent, and the ones who (can I say moan?) voice displeasure at yet another change, or 'Why are we bothering?' or 'Do they really expect me to do this?'

Educating your Super Users on all these natural reactions to change, and techniques to manage them, is important. You may have a change management team or lead already working with key and senior stakeholders – whereas the role here is for Super Users to work with end users. We need our Super Users to have a good understanding of applying change management principles, as they act here in the role of a change agent, and we need them to understand how to use ADKAR survey results to create an action plan to improve change acceptance in their own business functions.

See Chapter 8 for more on providing change education and ADKAR action plans.

Business processes

Your Super Users need to have time in their training programme to really study and learn the business process design done by your business process owners, consultants and analysts. The project team should be conducting sessions to walk a Super User through the 'As-Is' and 'To-Be' of a business process, explaining each step, the purpose and the desired output. As well as a process walkthrough, make sure Super Users are given the relevant business process documents and time to review them.

We have talked previously about how useful Super User feedback can be at this stage: let your Super Users give feedback and suggest changes to the design. Your project team are experts in the system design, but we recruited the Super Users for their expertise on performing the job in the real world; their contributions at this stage can be valuable and pay dividends later on in system adoption.

System familiarisation and navigation

The system may be brand new, or it may be just enhancements to a current system, but your Super Users need maximum exposure to the system at an early stage. It may be that your build or testing is not completed yet, but the Super Users need to be given familiarisation sessions on the user interface and how to navigate around the system before they learn a process in detail. Consider using the real test system or video demos on how it should work. Give them a session on navigation and what the system icons mean, but give them time to play on it too. Encourage them to just explore the system in a safe environment and click buttons to see what happens. (I love systems so much I do always call this 'playing'.)

Again, solicit Super User feedback here for finalising your design. Is the user interface built in such a way that it follows the logical sequence that an end user would do? Your Super Users can advise on this. Make sure they have their own login details to the test system so they can access it as and when required after this familiarisation session.

Test script writing

Here is the part where we educate the Super Users on testing. This is not running the tests, but the theory of testing. Conduct a session where they can understand the concepts of why we are testing – the objective is not to pass the tests, but to find the bugs. If you do not find them at this stage, then your end users will. Consider all possible scenarios that may happen in the real world: what happens if we do this or press this? Does the system give us the benefits we intended? Does the system work as intended and consistently? Does the system follow the business process design? Does the system make our end user roles easier to perform? Ensure both your testers and Super Users know this is why we test, and these are our real motivations.

If you are using any particular testing software, then they will need a familiarisation session here. If you are using Super Users to write test scripts, we can provide templates here and training on how to write a good test script. Ensure the script explains each required step and desired output. The script should advise what data and examples to use and how to record defects. A good test script should be able to be run by a complete novice to the system with no prior experience.

Once you have your test scripts, your Super Users would then need to plan the data they need to run each test. The earlier we prepare this the better. We need quality data with enough volume and variety to cover our planned testing. This may mean identifying data from a copy of your live system or you may need to add inventory or master data to your test system to cover your requirements.

Give them any other information here relevant to the testing stage: Are you categorising defects at capture stage? Who will resolve, who will retest and how? How many tests will there be, how many tests will each Super User write or execute? Where will we record test passes? Who will update the RTM? Consider having your testing lead run these sessions with your Super Users to really drive home the best practices of testing software in projects like these.

System expertise

System training must happen as close as possible to Go Live for your end users – but not for your Super Users. Your Super Users need to be shown the step-by-step process on the system as early as possible, preferably before testing starts (your testing team if you have one should be in these same sessions). This will involve a lot of sessions and the bulk of your training programme.

We want our Super Users to be experts on the system by the time we Go Live. This means they need to understand how the system was designed and why, how to navigate using all the icons and features, how to troubleshoot errors, and the most efficient ways to complete processes on the system. It is never just a matter of showing a Super User what buttons to press in which order so that they can pass those steps on to the end user a couple of weeks later. Give them time to learn the system processes, to practise (play) with the processes and to really become experts on how it should be done. This knowledge will become more reinforced as they run the test scripts and when they practise their end user delivery sessions – thus we are making them experts who stay in place after going live. A Super User is for the life of the system, not the life of the project. (I know I say that a lot, but I will keep doing it.)

You may need to consider assessing the strength and knowledge of your Super Users. This could be via competency testing or self-assessments; we need to ensure the Super Users have no further training requirements as well as making sure they are equipped to support your end users. Consider providing Super User certification at the completion of this stage, or a graduation ceremony to post about on your social media and company news. This will help with ensuring Super Users feel valued, but also ensuring your company knows who these Super Users are.

Executing test scripts

When you are ready to start your testing, a Super User will need refresher sessions on executing the tests. Ensure they know which tests they are expected to do, how to record passes or defects and how to classify a defect. Keep an eye on the completion rates of tests and offer support where needed.

Defects and retesting

Your Super Users as well as your project team need to be kept informed on the defects we have. They need to be given a good understanding of the defects relevant to their processes or end user departments. Ensure they know how a defect occurred – in case it comes up again after Go Live – and what was done to resolve it. Was a workaround put in place or a design changed? Your Super Users need to know this to remain experts on that system process. Use this part of the training schedule to give your Super Users the mechanisms to gain this knowledge, and to understand the processes around defect resolution, retesting and regression testing.

Train the trainer

Our next chapter explains the content for a train the trainer course in more detail. But now we have given the Super Users a system education, we need to develop their skills in training others. This is a skill all of its own and it does not matter what subject you are training on – systems or otherwise – there are particular skills that a trainer needs to have. Use these sessions to instil confidence in your Super Users, give them tips, have a say in the end user training design and devise a plan to let them practise their end user sessions.

Training materials

The training lead needs to ensure training materials are excellent quality, consistent and professional. Therefore, I would recommend they take the ownership for this and use the Super Users as a resource to populate and complete them. Give your Super Users sessions on how to complete and write training materials. But it needs to follow a consistent design or template that is provided. Give them a slide deck that they can amend; give them a template for an SOP, or step-by-step or quick reference guide; make sure they are following the same standards when using simple screen recording software.

I would recommend only your qualified training/L&D teams use an authoring tool (such as Captivate, Camtasia, Adobe Creative Suite, Vyond or Articulate). Super Users have enough already to make themselves experts on, but our Super Users can guide our training professionals to create high-quality content by acting as their SMEs and by providing a design specification.

Use this time in the training cycle to ensure all Super Users are committed to following the same guidelines and look and feel for any materials. Advise Super Users of their accountability for training materials: they need to consult, test and sign off any digital output from your training team; they need to ensure we have correct final versions of any materials for end users to use; they need to ensure they are loaded and accessible for users; and they need to be responsible for maintaining the accuracy after Go Live.

Practice delivery sessions

When you have finalised your end user training session plans, written your training materials and delivered your train the trainer courses, we need to create sessions where your Super Users practise delivering their end user sessions. Ensure your training lead attends as many personally as they can to give feedback on delivery techniques or to tweak session plans. Have your Super Users practise delivering to each other as well, and update session plans as they go along to ensure they remain correct. A good session plan should be able to be picked up by another trainer (who would have to know the system) at short notice and enable the session to be delivered as designed by someone else. We cover the session plan in more detail in the next chapter.

Support and escalation

You will have hopefully covered this with the support you have offered throughout the project, but I would recommend a session right before end user training starts to coordinate your Super Users. We need our Super User Lead to provide lots of guidance and support to Super Users prior to training delivery. Give them a checklist of what they need to do for each course: agendas or posters for the wall, slide decks ready, rooms booked, online breakout rooms organised, schedules agreed, invites sent, videos downloaded, handouts and evaluation forms ready, and many more tailored to your rollout. Your training team needs to stay connected with Super Users throughout this preparation stage to ensure everything is ready and to help with any obstacles or challenges along the way. Ensure they can report back to you the progress, completion of tasks and any obstacles they need assistance with. Ensure Super Users know how to report issues during the system training sessions, and who is on hand in IT to support remotely or on site. Have a similar session to this before your Go Live to coordinate where your Super Users will be, how they will report feedback and how they will escalate any issues and seek resolution.

Community meetings

I hope you have done this weekly or monthly since the project began, but have regular meetings or calls for your Super Users that includes training for them. Chapter 7 covered building the community but it is important to be mentioned here in the training programme too. Now you have this regular event with all your Super Users together, use this to pass on any system tips and to educate the Super Users on any new system features or advanced ways of working.

Personal development

A bit of a personal passion this one, but we know from when we discussed recruiting that we chose the best of the best to be Super Users and we know we have a group of people who can be used as a talent pool for the organisation. A bit of investment here in encouraging personal development can be huge for them as individuals, as well as creating high-performing teams for the business.

Share motivational videos and articles into your Super User groups and invite discussion. Host in-person or virtual watch parties to watch a TED talk together. Invite motivational speakers to events. Have a community library of self-help or business books, or have a book club for the project team and Super Users. Treat your Super Users as the talent they should be classed as, and encourage that continuous learning and improvement ethos. But not just personal development; instil the idea of continuous **professional** development into them as well; share those emerging technology demos, those agile explainer videos or articles on the best practices of testing.

Super User education model

Your Super Users will be receiving information, education and support from all the bubbles shown in Figure 11.1, which they will in turn pass on to end users. End users will also be receiving regular communications and strategic direction from both internal comms and our leadership. The flow of education needs to work as described in the model in Figure 11.1 to get the best results.

Figure 11.1 Super User education model

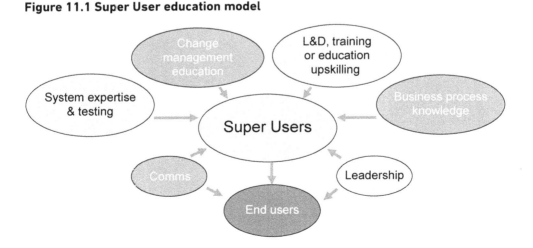

Final thoughts...

Super Users are learning throughout from onboarding to BAU. Keep them going with this concept and the business ends up with a talented, engaged and continually improving network of system and business experts. Honestly, hearing that, I have no idea why an organisation would ever not want to use a Super User Model.

12 HOW DO WE DELIVER A TRAIN THE TRAINER COURSE FOR SUPER USERS?

A recommended session plan to deliver a train the trainer course to Super Users, and the benefits of doing this.

Our train the trainer course for Super Users is going to be a condensed version of what it takes to be a successful trainer. So all those years of experience compacted into a one-day course – easy right? This course should not be about the system but about the skill of training, as it is likely your Super Users may not have trained end users in such a setting before.

Let us start with how we will teach them to start, with our objectives for the full day, face-to-face course. Deliver this course using all your best practice recommendations – the way you deliver the course is actually part of teaching them how they will deliver their course.

Course objectives

By the end of this course, Super Users will be able to:

- improve their confidence to deliver training;
- describe methods of engaging and managing course attendees;
- create a high-level session plan for training end users;
- agree suitable training methods for end user courses.

Mission and agenda

In a face-to-face course I like to have the mission, objectives and agenda printed or written on the walls or a flipchart, rather than on a presentation slide. This keeps it visible throughout the day, so attendees can see how we are progressing through the content and so that we can refer to it often as we check off completed activities. If it is virtual, make sure this information is provided in advance on the invites.

Use the mission statement we created in Chapter 8 to remind the team what we are hoping to achieve by implementing this system. It should be succinct enough to be on one poster or flipchart so that you can just read it out at the beginning to remind people of why we are here and the importance of it.

The agenda is then the structure of the day. What topics will you cover, when will you have breaks or lunch, what time are you hoping to finish? It helps to have this on display and for attendees to know this up front. However, a good trainer needs to be fluid with the agenda, and you may want to mention this concept to your audience. If you find your audience flagging after lunch, you may want to bring a break forward or throw in an extra activity. A discussion may be so useful it may go on longer than intended, or it may mean you have to cut it short or be prepared to make a certain section quicker or lose it altogether. It is not just important to get through all your content, it is more important to ensure attendees remain engaged throughout, so they are more likely to retain information and you are more likely to deliver on your objectives.

Confidence gauge

We can use this to measure the success of the course. Ask your attendees at the beginning and end of the course to rate their confidence level in delivering training; ensure you capture this to refer to later. It could be as simple as asking everyone to state their confidence level as a number out of 10 or you may want them to use an emoji chart like the one in Figure 12.1 and ask them to stick their name on a sticky note against the emoji they most identify with.

Figure 12.1 Delegate confidence gauge

Discussion on successful trainers

A discussion is a great way to start the course to get people warmed up and conversational. You can use light-hearted icebreakers; there are plenty on the internet or in other books, but I am more a fan of a focused discussion. We could ask, **What qualities make a successful trainer?** Because I'm super funny I like to throw in a joke there that a successful trainer is well dressed, intelligent and glamorous, you know... me. A bit of humour is good at the start of a course (as well as it being totally true). Ask people to call out traits that make a successful trainer and capture it on a flipchart or whiteboard. It is just a great way to open people up and have them thinking of who they need to be, to be good at delivering training. Therefore, it is not just about knowing the system inside and out (although of course I'm an expert at that too).

How to start a course

Do you know what no one wants to do in a training course? No one wants to come into a room and be talked at for hours while watching PowerPoint slide after slide. Therefore, we have not even opened our laptop by this stage. We've set the scene, we've hopefully had a few laughs, we've had a good discussion and we've enabled ourselves to have the best chances of an enjoyable day. At this point reiterate this back to your audience. Advise them to start with the 'why' and the 'how': the mission, the objectives and the agenda. Advise them to open people up with a discussion point at the beginning of the session – a good one for them to do with end users is ask them why we are changing or what they would like to change about their system or processes. But we need dynamic, engaging trainers so we do not rely on just slides, we get people comfortable to talk in the room, and we do not subject them to a long boring story of who the trainer is and what their background and experience is. (A side note, I feel the tendency for trainers to introduce themselves like that comes from imposter syndrome and proving why you are qualified to be there. Just believe it, and show it. Your previous experience is not necessary to include in the course.)

Funny video

At this point, I like to continue to create a warm room by showing a short funny video on how **not** to deliver a training course. You know the ones where the trainers are nervous and make lots of mistakes. There are a few on YouTube already or consider paying for content from a company such as Video Arts. After the video, conduct a brief discussion on what they saw that was incorrectly delivered. You may want to consider a break after this and then get your slides ready for the next section.

Training material options

We are now opening our slides and covering with the attendees all the options for them to consider when delivering training to end users; we want the Super Users to have a say in how end user training is delivered. Although it is possible that your L&D or education services team will produce certain material, make sure your Super Users are aware of all the options – they know the end users best and can suggest what will be the best option. Revisit the training material section from Chapter 10 to have a list of options. The final decision should be up to the training team, as they know the budget and resources available. But letting the Super Users be empowered to have a say in these decisions enhances their engagement and investment in success.

Training aids

You want your trainers to know that a course does not just have to be lots of slides and watching someone show you how to use the system. We want our courses to have different pace, different sections, different methods and hopefully a bit of fun. Use a slide or a discussion to advise them on different aids we can help them to have in their courses:

- laptops for attendees to click along with or complete activities on (you need a test system);
- flipchart/whiteboard;
- exercises and activities;
- animations and video;

- games (traditional or digital);
- props;
- music;
- room layout or online breakout rooms.

Training methods

Are your Super Users going to deliver classroom courses, virtual courses, elearning, workshops or supported practice sessions? Cover all the different methods you have available and let your Super Users be involved in deciding what is the best method. Introduce the concept of blended learning; maybe you will be able to do a bit of everything. But it is not just for the sake of it. Which methods do your Super Users think will be the best way for the end users to learn the new system?

Training strategy

One of my catchphrases for delivering system training is '**See It; Try It; Do It**.' This guides our blended learning programme to ensure end users receive a training method in each category. This is a way of reinforcing the actions or processes to aid retention, so here we present this technique to Super Users to consider in their training design (Figure 12.2).

Figure 12.2 IT systems training strategy

See it		Watch a video; see a live demonstration; read a user guide; have a trainer explain the process; see diagrams drawn of the process; hear a step-by-step walkthrough; watch a system demonstration.
Try it		Complete an elearning course; click along with the trainer on a practice system; complete activities on the practice system with support; competency checks.
Do it		Practise the processes on a test system; complete an assessment; feedback and competency coaching; on-the-job training and support.

This is apparent in Edgar Dale's cone of experience in Figure 12.3. This shows why it is important to have a blended learning experience, with a variety of materials and training aids, as learning the topic in a variety of ways means it is more likely to be remembered. This is also why I feel the Super Users should be heavily involved in designing the end user training experience, to not only aid their own learning but to get them invested in the success of the course.

Figure 12.3 Cone of experience (Source: Image adapted from: https://www.iconspng.com/image/94187/cone-of-experience-by-edgar-dale-text-converted-to-outlines, originally created by Edgar Dale)

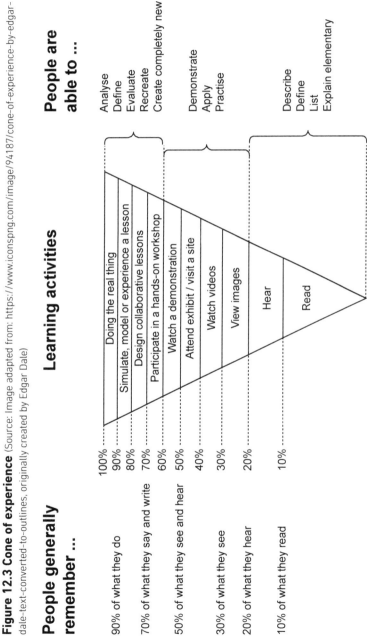

Delivery tips

Consider a role play to have Super Users presenting to each other on a subject they are passionate about and solicit feedback from their peers. Give them feedback on their tone of voice, their posture and body language, and how much they engaged directly with their audience.

Refer your Super Users to Chapter 14 of this book to cover specific advice on software training delivery that will be a big help to them here.

Managing delegates advice and activity

Advise them to encourage questions with their audience but not debate. Someone who is experiencing change resistance may derail your course by continually making negative comments. While you may want to assist the individual with this later you do not want this to go on too long. It is important when encountering this to **acknowledge** – **empathise** – then **move on**. We will make a note to pick this up in depth later though. We need to identify the most vocal resisters and plan to engage with them. They may have accurate insights we may have not considered, or if we win them over, they can help us influence others.

You can also make this into an activity, rather than lots of slides. Pair people up and give them each a scenario for them to advise the group how they would respond.

1. A delegate expresses frustration with a particular aspect of the system and is struggling to keep up with the rest of the group. What is your response?
2. During a group activity, one delegate attempts to take control and exclude others from participating. What is your response?
3. A group of delegates are visibly disengaged and uninterested in the training session. What is your response?
4. A delegate consistently interrupts others during the training session. What is your response?
5. A delegate arrives late to the training session and disrupts the flow of the session. What is your response?

Of course, there is no right and wrong response, so it is good to discuss recommended strategies as a group in case these come up. Let your training lead advise how they have handled it in the past. If one of your Super Users is showing these behaviours, you can even refer to it jokingly if you feel it will be well received and highlight what your response was to it.

Key mandatory points

There may be important key points specific to the project or a system process to reinforce to end users. Perhaps a required way to execute the process rather than the alternatives; or any desired new behaviours; or the importance of doing tasks on the system at particular times. If there is something you know as the trainer or system expert to be crucial, ensure you tell your Super Users the points that **must** be in their end user sessions, that are not optional to mention.

Group activity: session planning

Now you've given your Super Users lots of ideas as to how they can deliver this system training, and with a view to keeping them involved in the training design, we can now include another activity by having them design the end user training session plan (see Table 12.1).

Table 12.1 Session plan example

Name of course:

Course objectives:

Session details: Date, location, trainers, attendees, resources (e.g. laptops, flipcharts)

Course overview: High-level overview of agenda, training media and materials, training methods, evaluation method

Course preparation: Room layout, webinar programme, invites, exercises, signage, catering booked

Pre-work: e.g. online course/PDF to read

Course detail:

Timing	Topic & sub-topics	Key messages	Media/method/ resource	Evaluation method
9–9.30	Introduction	Importance of new system	Video from sponsor	N/A
9.30–10	Topic 1		Presentation	
10–10.30	Topic 1 • Log in • Navigation • Search for customer		System demo	
10.30	Break			
10.50	Topic 1		System practice	• Observations • Exercises • Knowledge check

Continues through to end of course

Split your group into two or more teams and ask them to draft a session plan for different processes, topics or modules. Show them an example of a session plan (perhaps your session plan for this course) or give them a template. Give them 45 minutes or more to produce a draft of how they would deliver an end user course: consider pre-work; materials; training methods and aids; activities; quizzes; sequence of topics; time allowed for each topic; breaks and so on.

They can either then present this back to the group afterwards or submit them for you to review later. Bear in mind with delivering this course multiple times you will have a few to review when finalising your session plan design. This helps you to know you have the final decision in session design but also ensures the Super Users have had a collaborative approach to the end user courses. Acknowledge the Super Users' contribution at a later date when you distribute the final session plans.

Next steps

Ensure Super Users are aware of the next steps following completion of this train the trainer course. That you will finalise session plans, that they will receive system familiarisation sessions if that has not already started, that we will schedule for them to practise delivering sessions and to receive feedback, and ensure they know how they will be supported throughout the entire process.

Confidence gauge

Do not forget to refer to your confidence gauge from the beginning of the course – try to do this in a way you can capture to measure the success of your delivery. Have your Super Users changed their number rating, or emoji position by the end of the course? Always ask them how you can assist them next to further enhance their confidence. Make a note of these requests and try to deliver on their suggestions (more practice sessions for example) to help them further.

Review objectives

Revisit your objectives to remind them of what we have covered during the day and what we have achieved – using the opportunity to reinforce key messages if needed. Remind people to do this in their own end user courses.

13 HOW DO WE DESIGN ELEARNING FOR SOFTWARE TRAINING?

Recommendations for digital learning content creation – specific to providing training for software applications.

You cannot learn how to use a complex system from elearning alone. But it does have a place in a blended learning programme to reinforce aspects of it. Let us revisit '**See It; Try It; Do It**' from our last chapter.

You can utilise digital learning to provide the '**See It**' part of systems instruction, such as a video demo or recorded webinar.

You can use a system simulation in elearning or guided instructional exercises on your training system, to cover the '**Try It**' phase.

You can provide prebuilt exercises, assessments or instructions in a training system for independent practice for the '**Do It**' phase.

Show a brief demonstration on a video first, and then have a system simulation. Basically, recreate your software screens (Adobe Captivate is better than Articulate for this in my opinion) and advise them to click the same steps they saw in the video. Use hint prompts for where they click that only appear after a timed delay and provide feedback for wrong clicks. It is better to allow the learner to work this out, with hints if they do not remember a step, rather than just following 'click here, click there' instructions. This works much better when your system has an intuitive interface (another reason why we, and our Super Users need to be involved in the system configuration and design, particularly when discussing the user experience (UX)).

Ideally you will have a training or test system for users to practise an exercise on; make sure you show step-by-step instructions with screenshots or short videos showing a task at a time. This is a better experience than a long video that a user may have to pause and rewind to get the information they need to complete the exercise.

We can then use some interactions to assess or reinforce knowledge. Think quizzes, drag and drop, fill in the blanks type questions. Perhaps show a screen and use 'hot spots' to see if the learner can remember where to click. Or something more innovative. If you have the tools, a factor that provides intrinsic motivation is giving comparative scores, such as 'You Scored Higher Than 85% of Participants'. This encourages learners to retake assessments to get a higher score, further reinforcing their learning, and if this is a series of assessments it motivates them to continue.

If you are using narration, it is fine to use a speech to text or AI generated voiceover for narrative, instructional or descriptive text. However, the technology needs to be good enough to project real personality, enthusiasm and tonality for a human voice. If you can record decent quality audio to use, then do this, but if you use technology to generate audio for conversational dialogue, it needs to sound like a human. For production speed, there is nothing wrong with recording a screen demonstration while you are speaking over it, and having your webcam on while you are doing this helps to make it more of a human-to-human interaction, which our brain prefers. Recorded screen demos are still adequate for system training purposes; they appear authentic and are much easier to replace when there are changes.

If you are using video for system training, then a series of micro-learning videos is the way to go. Particularly if we expect users to need to watch the video again when they are actually performing the task. Keep them short and simple, covering one task at a time. If you must do a longer video, consider adding bookmarks or text with the timestamp of particular topics or tasks.

Always consider accessibility and inclusion in your elearning design. This is why a blended learning programme is always best so people have options in how they consume the training; but we should still incorporate best practice recommendations when creating content. This includes alt-text descriptions added to any images; make sure any documents we create can be read by a screen reader and are logically laid out in a manner that helps comprehension such as section headings; include closed captions on our videos or transcripts on our webinars; while we should take care to not have too many words on a screen at once, users should also have zoom and full-screen features to deploy; and finally, consider the colours you use by using a colour contrast checker or investigate if dark modes are an option.

Similarly, consider if your design needs to be responsive to adapt to different screen sizes, but use data to determine this. Would many people take your course on phones or tablets, or is it all from a desk?

No one likes long, boring elearning courses anymore; it is not just 'death by PowerPoint' we experience in the corporate world, but it's 'death by next button' too. Make sure you separate a course of lessons into manageable chunks of micro-learning; create a lesson per task and create a curriculum or learning plan of all the lessons required for each role – rather than one lengthy course.

Use storytelling in your elearning, create character-led and situational scenarios with a real-life contextual trigger such as simulating a customer call or chat message. Consider animation or videos for setting up the role play part of the elearning before moving on to the software procedure. Giving people an onscreen timer works well with this too: can they complete the task before the customer gets impatient, with points for speed and accuracy. One other thing that works for storytelling and context – memes. If you can find a suitable, content appropriate meme then add it in for humour, and it really helps to make the situation relatable.

A fun storyboarding process I have learned to bring in storytelling aspects is to research the concept of 'The Hero's Journey'; it's a really good framework to map your content against, one you will recognise from many books and films. Think *Star Wars* or *Harry Potter*. The Hero's Journey structure for storytelling typically involves starting in an ordinary world, receiving a call to action, facing challenges to overcome, learning important lessons, and enlisting allies (such as your Super Users) before ultimately reaping the rewards in a new and transformed world. Assess how you can map your elearning storyboard against this structure.

One of the most fun projects I have been involved in was an online training needs analysis. It was designed to assess a group of 400 people to determine whether they had the correct soft skills for dealing with a customer complaint in line with policy: did they understand the correct process and could they perform the task on the system? It could have been done with boring competency assessments, surveys, self-scoring matrixes or making them sit through the same complaints training they had done before. But we did it a different way.

We made it into a game with a leaderboard and prizes for the highest scorers (extrinsic motivation). Each task they passed gave them a part of a retro game, based on Tetris and Mario and Space Invaders – so that if they obtained all the pieces they needed, they could play a Tetris level. We used animation and funny skits, with voices recorded by our senior board members, to assess which option they thought was the best verbal response to a complaint. We used multiple choice questions, some in the style of *Jeopardy* and *Who Wants To Be a Millionaire*, and other drag and drop features to determine whether they understood the process steps they should follow. And we used a point scoring system simulation to assess whether they knew how to raise returns, refunds or log complaints on the system within a certain time limit.

We never made it mandatory but by creating a buzz around the scores on our social network and in team meetings we got a 92% completion rate. It served a purpose to reinforce the correct procedures to the teams but the end result from our fun elearning was a very formal detailed report using Sharable Content Object Reference Model (SCORM) outputs. This reported to stakeholders and department heads showing at a department, team and individual level where our training needs and gaps were, and what personalised training plan each person needed.

It is also worth pointing out that actually all we were asked to do was to rerun the complaints system training with the customer service function, but we questioned whether that was the answer to their problem. Actually, the results showed they understood the system most of all, but what we needed was more communication from senior management on what the complaints policies were for different scenarios.

Creating engaging courses is the goal here though, not 'fun'. Even with the most enjoyable jobs, we are not at work because it is fun. eLearning can be entertaining, but most of all, it should be educational. Do not introduce gamification elements for the sake of it; each interaction should serve a purpose. Consider that your learners are adult professionals. Are they likely to feel patronised when your course makes them take a rocket ship to the moon? Is it getting in the way of what performance support they need to actually just get on with their job? They are busy people – start with the objectives of what they need to be able to do after the course, then add only necessary information and interactions on top of this. If you have not already done so, go and read Cathy Moore's action mapping[3] before you create your learning design. 'Best way to respect learners: Use techniques that research has proven to work. Help people reach their goals without wasting their time.'[4]

Work with your instructional designers to plan the best solution for the time, skills and tools you have. Talk with them about the various levels of elearning and what would make the best experience.

- **Passive**: Video or slides to consume only. The just watch or 'click next' style of elearning.
- **Interactive**: These courses are informational with some click and reveal interactions and knowledge checks added.
- **Complex:** This has more complex gamification, with scenario-based branching, storytelling or more innovative interactions.
- **Immersive**: A full immersive course embeds the user in a contextual story, with elements of all the previous levels, but containing personalisation, feedback, consequences and real-time learning of actions and choices.

You should also consider adding gamification to the launch of your new system. Assign points for completing activities and regularly advertise the winning teams. Activities could include having installed the software and logged in, all elearning or assigned courses completed, all team members certified to have completed their training or the first business process (order, shipment, invoice, etc.) has been executed. Additional points could be given for posting or responding to community threads, or engaging in any competitions, quizzes, crosswords, hackathons or other interactions. Offer a good team prize for this incentive.

eLearning absolutely can still play a constructive part in system training. But we are not just training them how to use a system; we want them to fully adopt the software and technology. To do this, it is not just about providing training before we Go Live. We need to provide a continuous learning experience. This is partly done by keeping our Super Users in place cascading out refresher training, giving best practice advice, or with training aids or short videos that can be consumed at the time of the task. However, there is another digital strategy to consider.

Digital adoption platforms (DAPs) that provide 'in-app' training are a great solution to look at. When the staff member or customer is using your software and needs training support, is it better for them to leave the screen and go and log into an LMS or portal to take an elearning course, or to spend time searching a folder or system for the PDF of the instructions? Or alternatively, is it better for them to click a button on the screen they were already in, to launch a step-by-step walkthrough, wizard or 'How-To' video? Give them real 'at the point of need' training support. If you have the budget and time to

3   Moore. C. (no date) *Action mapping on one page.* Cathy Moore Blog. https://blog.cathy-moore.com/online-learning-conference-anti-handout/

4   Farrell, L. (2021) *Training & development quotes to motivate your L&D team.* Cognota. https://cognota.com/blog/training-and-development-quotes-to-motivate-your-ld-team/

explore a DAP, it is highly recommended, and you can use it for multiple systems and websites in your organisation.

The future for systems training in my opinion needs to be travelling in this direction. Your LMS, university or online academy will always have a place for onboarding and skills development, but in educating users how to use a digital product, the 'training' should be right there in the product within an intuitive user interface.

Questions to ask:

Do I have a blended programme covering all aspects of 'See It; Try It; Do It'? (If no, recommend other methods are considered in addition to the required elearning.)

Do I have a training system I can use or can I build a system simulation to enable a user to practise?

Do I have the design agreed (e.g. video, elearning, ebook)?

Do I have the level of interactivity agreed (e.g. passive to immersive)?

Do I have the required skill in my team to create graphics, courses or interactions or do I need to source external instructional designers?

Have I considered accessibility and inclusivity?

Do I have knowledge checks, assessments or examinations in place?

Is all the information and interactivity in the course supporting the objectives? (If no, consider removing to keep the course focused.)

Have I applied real-life context, scenarios or analogies to the course?

Can I use gamification within this course?

Can I use gamification with a team prize for the launch of the software?

Can I use DAP software or in-house developers to generate training support embedded within the software interface?

14 HOW DO WE DELIVER SOFTWARE TRAINING?

The recommended delivery techniques for both virtual and in-person classroom training, and how software training delivery should differ from traditional training.

Our Super Users are responsible for delivering the training on our new software to the end users, and we have worked together in our train the trainer course to create a session plan detailing activities, methods and timings. We have also arranged for our Super Users to practise delivering that session plan.

This chapter will cover specific tips on how to successfully deliver that end user training, for us to use and for our Super Users. Perhaps giving each of your Super Users a copy of this book would be helpful and a worthwhile investment in their development.

Training professionals have likely delivered other courses before: think health and safety, product training, maybe customer service training or personal development. But we do need to treat software training slightly differently.

GENERAL DELIVERY TIPS

1. Remember we start the first training session with a 'Why': why we are using this software; why we are undergoing this organisational change; why it is important for them to have the training; why we're executing the new process in a particular way. Strongly recommend this is delivered by the CEO or project sponsor, with a branded video message if not personally attending.

2. Set expectations for questions: are they free to ask questions throughout (recommended) or should they wait till the formal Q&A section? If online can they put the questions in chat in advance for this?

3. We need to plan in additional breaks, more than you would have in a 'normal' course. It does not necessarily have to be all refreshment or lunch breaks, it may be a break from the screen for a discussion, but we cannot have delegates staring at a screen or concentrating on screen demos for an extensive amount of time. It is draining, and not effective for learning. Remember, hydrated students are alert students.

4. If possible, have more than one facilitator, whether online or in person. One person can present or take it in turns to present. The other person can then monitor the online chat, provide resources in chat or handouts, manage timekeeping, give personal attention if needed, manage breakout rooms, provide IT support, or do floor walking to have an eye on those who need additional support or may have questions.

5. Cognitive overload needs considering. The human brain and working memory can only take in so much new information at once. This means that you cannot plan to have all the information imparted in one session – it may need several. In the session, whether it is one or more, we need to work on building up the information in an easy to consume manner. Give information in micro chunks, ensure that it is understood, then practised, then reinforced before moving on to any new topic.

6. Remember the '**See It; Try It; Do It**' technique from Chapter 12. I often like to have a separate session in advance for the '**See It**'. Provide them with an overview session with just a demo and answer any questions. This allows people to process that, and helps with their change management curve, before in a later session we can allow them to have hands-on practice, stepping through as you guide them click by click (**Try It**) and then giving them some independent exercises and practice sessions as well as Go Live support (**Do It**).

7. Consider the **VARK** (visual, aural, read, kinaesthetic) model in your training design to reinforce learning by conveying the information in different ways.

   a. **V**isual: This could be a diagram of how the system works; or a process flow.

   b. **A**ural: This could be an explanation or a discussion, or even a podcast to listen to as pre- or post-work.

   c. **R**ead/Write: This can be handouts or guides for the delegates to read and consult. Encourage note taking for the writing aspect.

   d. **K**inaesthetic: This is the hands-on aspect. By providing practice sessions, test systems, assessments and drop-in rooms we can cater for this learning preference. But by providing elements of all these learning styles, we are enabling the different parts of the brain to absorb the information in multiple ways, thus aiding the recall potential.

8. I do hope you have read this somewhere else before this book, but if you are using PowerPoint slides remember they are there only as the support act; you are the expert star of the show. Do not have slides with every word you are going to say on them; training professionals **do not** read from slides. We can use images or diagrams to support our points, we can use bullet points or quotes to reinforce what we are saying – but too often in the past slide decks have been used as a presenter script. This is due to the redundancy principle: we either let our learners read the slide, or listen to what we say, but we do not do both concurrently; this is not conducive to the learning process or our reputation.

9. Similarly, we do not always need to have slides constantly on. Draw something out on a whiteboard (physical or virtual), switch the slides off and you be centre stage (in person or using your video), or consider using physical flash cards or even props to make your point.

10. In our training plan we specified our course objectives, and set the competency level in our learning needs analysis. Allow this to guide you when determining the level of detail and effort you go into in your teaching, and to not overwhelm your learners unnecessarily. Remember the Three E's of Competency: Are you teaching **essentials, efficiency or excellence**?

11. Break up your training sessions into a flow of changing modality. A recommended flow is:

a. presenting and discussion;

b. video or animation of concepts, vision, the system or its benefits;

c. live demonstration;

d. guided 'click by click' exercise;

e. break;

f. summarise key points;

g. practice or exercise;

h. break;

i. interactions: role plays; polls; Q&A; brainstorming (in person or with annotation or dedicated software) or a discussion;

j. knowledge check; quiz or assessment;

k. break;

l. and repeat for next topic.

12. Alternatively, consider **Gagné's Nine Events of Instruction** as a format for your session plan:

    i. Gain attention of the students.

    ii. Inform students of the objectives.

    iii. Stimulate recall of prior learning.

    iv. Present the content.

    v. Provide learning guidance.

    vi. Elicit performance (practice).

    vii. Provide feedback.

    viii. Assess performance.

    ix. Enhance retention and transfer.

13. When providing a system demonstration, remember that a lot of people will find it hard to take notes at the same time as following and remembering the steps. It is best to demo a system process twice, the first time make it clear they are just to watch, and you can do this in real-time speed as you would in a real setting. The second time enable them to take notes (either freehand or on any handouts) and you can do this a little slower with more explanation. Set the expectation that this is just passive for them at first; they shouldn't be on the system themselves yet when watching a demo. We will next be clicking through the process together so advise them they will get on the system then. That expectation relieves anxiety and keeps them informed how they will learn.

14. Try to explain your demonstrations with a real-life scenario, with context for their particular roles. It is not just teaching them to press buttons, it is telling a story as to why they would, what impact it has, and what other processes it triggers.

15. Summarise repeatedly after each topic and after each break – reinforce key points to encourage retention.

16. Conclude any sessions by being clear on what happens next: How can they learn more independently if they wish? What other courses will they need to do? Where do they go to find the training resources? Who do they direct any questions to? How will we communicate any follow-ups to them (if a question wasn't answered in the session)? What key dates do they need to know? What is the IT support model for Go Live? Who are their Super Users?

An example of storytelling I have applied in courses, is to take advantage of popular recent events. In a sales training course when I needed to teach people how to use a pricing system to create a quote and decide on a pricing point, I utilised recent footage of Stormzy, and another time Ed Sheeran, performing at Glastonbury. We viewed them as the customer and provided a quote, price, email and follow-up appointment to sell Ed his boots and to sell Stormzy his infamous Banksy vest. It made the course a little more interesting than just 'press these buttons to create this quote', it provided role play opportunities, a bit of fun when they were asked to spot when I slipped in lyrics from their music into my talking points that day, and finally, it was just great to watch a bit of Glastonbury in the middle of the work day.

TIPS FOR CLASSROOM TRAINING

1. Utilise all the space you have. There is no rule that says the presenter can only be at the front of the classroom or behind a lectern. Have pre-written process flows on the walls you can move to when you need to explain that section. Move to your whiteboard or flipchart when you need to.

2. If you need breakout rooms, make sure in advance your venue can facilitate that and set up those spaces beforehand.

3. Bring gamification into the classroom. Provide sweets or prizes to give out if they answer some quick-fire questions. Split the room in half and ask them to write questions to quiz each other on – with a prize for the winning team of course. It would be great here to have a leaderboard for the winning team if you are planning more than one of these, or if the course runs over a few days. Kahoot! or similar tools are an enjoyable way of interacting in the classroom, providing them with a quiz to do from their mobile phones in the session.

4. Consider laptop management. Make sure they all have a safe (no trailing wires) power source. Provide usernames and passwords for both the laptop and the software. Check in with IT that no updates are planned during your course.

5. Ensure you know the mechanism of connecting to any screens, conferencing or audio equipment in the room.

6. Make sure you choose an accessible venue and consider travel arrangements. If necessary, provide an online link for remote workers or record your event so those who cannot attend can watch later.

7. If it is an all-day course, please do provide both refreshments and lunch. Not only does keeping them hydrated and fed aid their learning capability, but it is only right and fair too. Plus, if you allow them to go off-site for their own lunch, inevitably someone will be late back and disrupt your flow.

8. You need to make it simple for people to have smoke breaks, regardless of your personal feelings on smoking. Not being able to smoke will provide stress, which is not conducive to learning. Make sure they know where to go, and any safety considerations such as wearing a high-vis vest. Give them enough time to be able to eat, go to the bathroom and to get to the smoking area and back comfortably.

9. How to win friends and influence people? Let them leave training courses early. If they are meant to usually work till 5 p.m., plan to let them leave no later than 4.30 p.m. It is a draining day already; please do not have them sat there tired watching the clock until that metaphorical bell rings for the end of the day. An all-day course should be no more than six hours, with no more than four hours of that being listening to delivery or watching a screen.

TIPS FOR VIRTUAL TRAINING

1. Don't just be a voice; put your webcam on. Use eye contact, gestures and body language to project enthusiasm the same as you would in a classroom. The scientific evidence is there that we communicate more effectively that way. Different parts of the brain are then receiving the information simultaneously. This does not just mean having your video switched on in meetings, it means you need to look directly at the camera lens that is focusing on you. This may mean altering your setup, so a webcam is on the monitor instead of using the one built into your laptop. Consider stopping screenshare at certain points, so your face is the focus rather than your screen. Attendees are then more likely to engage and watch, rather than sit listening while simultaneously checking their email.

2. Have a tidy uncluttered background or blur your surroundings, or use a professional picture background. No one is expecting you in a suit and tie anymore, well hopefully not in this day and age, but make yourself presentable.

3. Join five minutes in advance so you can use that time to welcome and chat to people. Do not wait for people to join if the majority of people are there on time.

4. If joining the webinar requires several steps, such as downloading software, make sure you have provided instructions in your invite and set an earlier start time.

5. Record your session so you can provide this to anyone who could not attend or joined late. You can also use this as content for your LMS.

6. Utilise tools for interactivity in your sessions. There are lots of software options to explore such as Miro, Slido, Lucidchart, Kahoot! again or Mentimeter. But even Microsoft Teams and Zoom have excellent features you can use.

7. Practice your webinar tools in advance, and do not worry as we have all forgotten to unmute ourselves at one point, but just remember to check.

8. Test the software you are training on as close as possible to the start time. Well actually a little bit in advance might help if there is an issue; I have been on the

phone to my IT support once with 18 minutes to go before a session started and they had to fix my software access just in time. Thanks Mike and Dave.

9. Consider playing music or displaying a countdown timer for breaks; this will help to ensure people are ready to go when you are.

10. Use polling and chat features to ask for feedback at the end. Getting feedback within the session is best, but if not, provide a survey link as soon as possible afterwards. Training professionals evaluate and use data to improve on every learning intervention they deliver.

11. In this working at home age, check your children have their snacks, cartoons, YouTube, that they have everything they need before you start. Ask them not to interrupt you. However, if they do, don't panic. There will be many working parents on your course watching you and empathising with the situation. Calmly deal with it, with good humour, and send them on their way again. You can scold them after the call.

12. I am so torn on this last one. There is nothing that brightens my day more than seeing a cat or dog unexpectedly appear on my screen on a colleague's video. But they are disruptive. From experience, I shut my cats away or I will invariably end up with a cat on my shoulder at some point. And how is it a cat only has to walk across your keyboard briefly and they have changed the zoom, opened programs you didn't know you had and sent a gibberish email to the boss?

15 HOW DO WE EVALUATE THE TRAINING STRATEGY AND USER ADOPTION?

The recommended approach to evaluate the training, the organisational culture, the software solution and the user maturity.

How do we evaluate training? We send a survey out, or pass out a 'happy sheet', and we ask them if they enjoyed the course and to rate their trainer. Then we pat ourselves on the back and move on. Right? We have all seen this approach many times. But there is no point in doing any kind of evaluation unless you plan to do something with the data. Do not add evaluation to your project or training plan to check the box; ensure a period is also marked out to analyse, interpret and create actions from the findings.

In this chapter we will look at how we evaluate our training, but not only that, it is important to evaluate our software product too, our company culture and our users via a maturity model. This gives us the whole picture on whether we are adopting the technology, and whether the technology is meeting its stated business aims and contributing to the success of company objectives. If not, why are we doing it?

EVALUATING TRAINING

There are many models for evaluating training, but the most suitable for our purposes is the Kirkpatrick Model (Figure 15.1). We will explore some evaluation ideas for each level of the model next.

Figure 15.1 Kirkpatrick Evaluation Model (Source: Image adapted from: Kirkpatrick Partners, Free Resources: https://www.kirkpatrickpartners.com/resources/)

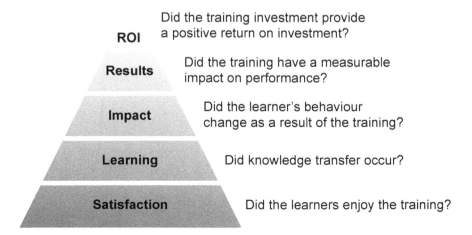

ROI — Did the training investment provide a positive return on investment?

Results — Did the training have a measurable impact on performance?

Impact — Did the learner's behaviour change as a result of the training?

Learning — Did knowledge transfer occur?

Satisfaction — Did the learners enjoy the training?

Satisfaction

Did the learners enjoy the training?

Ideas:

- Simply ask them if they enjoyed it:
  - If it is a multiple day course, ask them at the end of the first day as you may be able to adapt the style or pace for the second day.
  - Record or note the responses.
- Use a sticky note or sticker chart:
  - Mount a flipchart with a pre-written scale of enjoyment, confidence or usefulness, and ask them to position themselves on it using labelled pins or sticky notes.
  - They can write any comments or feedback down and stick them on the provided poster.
- Provide a paper or online survey:
  - A scale of 1–4 for ratings is always better than 1–5. This avoids the user being able to choose the middle ground of 3, which gives us no real indication of how we are doing.
  - The survey should be able to be completed quickly, only asking for the key information.
  - Do not make every comment field mandatory, as this can be a frustrating experience to have to add comments for every question. Leave most comment fields as optional with one general comment field mandatory to encourage more qualitative feedback.
- Use an iPad in the room with a simple click screen to use on their way out.
- Use online polls in the virtual meeting.
- Use digital star ratings in an online course.
- If any responses indicate they did not enjoy the training, consider if you can deliver further sessions or reflect on what we can improve next time.

Learning

Did knowledge transfer occur?

Ideas:

- Again, simply ask them.
- Provide a quiz, test or assessment.
- Could they complete the training exercises on the system?
- Do an observed competency assessment.

- Monitor the elearning pass rates.

- Provide self-assessments for them to rate their knowledge.

- If any responses indicate they did not learn from the training, it is important to dig deeper to find out why. You must follow up with either amended materials, further sessions or more concentrated Super User support.

Impact

Did the learner's behaviour change as a result of the training?

Ideas:

- Host a feedback forum.

- Interview managers or attendees of the training.

- Random system checks – are people using the system as trained?

- Consider process mining technology to compare actual process taken versus the official standard process or way of working.

- Use a chat board (anonymous or otherwise) to prompt answers or feedback.

- Consider any change in feedback provided by external sources such as customers.

- Spend time in the impacted departments to observe behaviours or ways of working.

- Export data from your system to look for adherence to trained methods.

- If any responses indicate behaviours did not change, again dig deeper as to why, and consider what other interventions are needed from us or from leadership to address this.

Results

Did the training have a measurable impact on performance?

Ideas:

- Check your original business case for the stated metrics or benefits.
  - Establish reporting to measure costs saved, revenue earned, hours saved and so on, or proof of progress against expected metric.

- Are service level agreements being met?

- Do a time study to compare the before and after of executing the process in the new system versus the old.

- Measure the number of errors (with cause analysis).

- Key performance indicator (KPI) performance.

- Number of helpdesk requests.

- Number of Super User help requests.

- Data on course pass rate, completion rate or number of views.

- Employee satisfaction ratings (only questions that are relevant to having the right system tools to do their job or training and knowledge to follow the business processes they use).

- Changes in customer satisfaction rating or customer effort score.

- Consider tools for data analytics and insights, or learning experience application programming interfaces (xAPIs) to measure real-time user experience of courses. (Such as were slides or videos skipped? Are they too long, irrelevant?)

- If any responses indicate negative or declining results, work with the relevant experts to create an action plan to improve on the reported metrics.

Return on investment (ROI)

Did the training provide a positive return on investment?

Ideas:

- Measure ROI% using the following formula:

$$\frac{(\text{Benefits} - \text{Cost of Training})}{\text{Cost Training}} \times 100 = \text{ROI\%}$$

- Cost of training could include venue or material costs, accommodation and hospitality, staff salary in time to build, consultancy costs, investment in any training tools, licensing costs, marketing costs and more.

- Consider revenue impact, for example having salespeople attending training and not out generating sales.

- Measure value of time saved: actual versus expected versus projected for future.

- Impact on helpdesk support. (Savings as it prevents tickets? Or costs because of increased demand?)

- Impact on staff retention.

- Evidence of impact on employee morale.

- Contribution to company objectives.

- If any responses indicate we have not seen a positive return on investment, draft a report justifying why, or do an exercise to forecast when we will see savings or improvements and consider lessons learned for the next project.

ADKAR RATINGS

Revisit the change management plan chapter on how useful it is to use the Prosci ADKAR® model. Following your training and following Go Live, do not forget to follow up with surveys on the knowledge, ability and reinforcement categories.

Use colour coding for team or department results to show whether they indicate positive or negative ratings. As with all evaluation data, work with your experts and Super Users to initiate an action plan on what needs to happen next to improve those scores and get everyone as green as you can. Doing nothing at this stage will only result in further declining scores; they will not improve on their own. Remember to measure again following completion of your action plan, and after a significant time lapse, to enable those changes to have effect.

EVALUATING SYSTEM ADOPTION

We need to establish some digital adoption metrics. To be clear, this should not be an L&D or Super User responsibility, but we need to ensure it is being done by someone.

What if the training was brilliantly planned and executed, but the system just is not doing what it was designed for? Or is it that the system is brilliant, but the training did not do it justice? We need to know this information to deal with the impact of either one.

The following list covers suggestions of factors that we may want to measure or determine, to give us an idea of how likely we are to fully adopt the system.

- Is the system performing as designed?
- Is the system meeting KPIs and aligned with company objectives?
- Are the numbers of errors and outages within expected and acceptable levels?
- Are the issues being resolved within an expected and acceptable timescale?
- Are users logging in, with the frequency and time spent in the system as expected?
- Are we using all the licences we expected?
- What is the net promoter or customer satisfaction score for the software?
- What are the daily, weekly and monthly active users?
- What are the results of any UX studies to assess user interface and ease of use?
- Do Super Users have the required advanced expertise to support people?
- Does the system have the adaptability to respond to future internal and external changes?
- How difficult is the system to administer by IT?
- Do Super Users require any additional permissions?
- Is the system capable of scalable growth as the company grows?
- Is the system compatible to integrate with your other systems?
- Is the system safe and secure for data and compliance?
- Where is the system development on the scale of standard to bespoke? What future impact could that have?

- Are there a number of workarounds in place, or are users finding it easy to use the system and processes as designed?

- Do we have a healthy pipeline for enhancements or ideation for the software?

- Have the users stopped using any old legacy software? Have we turned off access?

- Do users feel the new system is better than the old system?

EVALUATING COMPANY CULTURE

We need human resources (HR), organisational change management (OCM) or organisational design colleagues to consult on the culture of the organisation, to provide the right working environment conducive to technology adoption.

- Does the company have the right culture in place to promote a digital mindset and embrace change?

- Are people managers driving adoption of the technology?

- Are leaders enabling the conditions for the change and project to embed?

Culture is hugely important in driving any digital transformation, and that is not something you can dictate, but how people feel the organisation 'is'. It is the values and behaviours that determine how things happen. Does the CEO or board expect to deliver top-down mandates and it just gets done? Or, the one we need, do they lead by creating a compelling case to accept why we need to change and inspire people to make it happen?

One example I have seen where culture played a part, was an implementation of a new HR performance management and compensation system. The change was met with distrust from a significant number of staff. They were unsure of the purpose of the change and sceptical of the motives behind it. They felt it was to be a tool to micromanage them, to pick fault not praise, to give management tools to avoid giving pay rises or paying overtime. That does not come from nowhere; there have been managers making them feel that way in the past. Forcing the new system on them amid that sentiment would not have generated organic employee engagement or adoption.

Yes, they may have used the system because they were told to, but what is the objective of using a performance management system: to create high-performing teams. An external consultant was brought in to analyse the culture of the business before generating a change and comms campaign for the new HR system as well as some other changes. The consultant found stark differences in how some departments felt about where they worked, and about bringing in the new systems and ways of working.

The departments that welcomed the change had very similar things in common (they were trusted to do their jobs, they were treated like adults, they were judged on outputs not hours at a desk, they were consulted and involved in decision making, and they felt mentored and well-treated by their managers). Overall, they worked in departments that valued employee experience. If this was only present in some departments, not all, this feeling had been generated by some good managers and not the company culture. We could push ahead with implementing the new system, or we could work with the board and leaders from other areas first to educate managers on the culture we wanted to have, and focus on creating values and behaviours around a positive employee experience. This then supported the aims of the project and the system, as well as benefiting the whole company.

EVALUATING USER MATURITY

This should be conducted as a continual exercise. Map your users as to where they sit on the maturity model shown in Table 15.1 and consider how you move them through the Three E's of Competency.

This can be an activity given to each Super User to do for their own areas, at regular intervals, with an action plan per team. Follow up with your Super Users to give them accountability for this important part of the evaluation.

This shows why a Super User presence is required to build on the knowledge and competency of users over time. I would also recommend using the results of this to ensure you have succession planning in place for your Super User roles.

Table 15.1 User maturity model

User level	System expertise	Competency level
New user	• Understands basic functions and navigation • Requires training support and guidance to use the system for their role	Essential
Developing user	• Can execute system processes with occasional dependence on training support	
Operational user	• Can routinely execute system processes with support only required for unexpected issues	Efficient
Thriving user	• Has an advanced knowledge of the system and can train others • Potential Super User	Excellence
Super User	• Recognised system expert actively supporting end users • Promotes best practice standards and process execution	

PRESENT YOUR FINDINGS AND RECOMMENDATIONS

Complete a formal presentation or report on all of the above for your project sponsor, project managers, key stakeholders and impacted department heads. Include recommendations on what we do next. Justify why and get their buy-in to implement your proposed action plan.

Present your progress on evaluations at regular intervals. I would suggest doing this one month after Go Live, three months, six months and then 12 months to show the progress and benefits realisation.

Who owns the evaluation?

Kirkpatrick Method of evaluating training: training or Super User Lead.

ADKAR Method of evaluating change acceptance: OCM or Super User Lead.

Software solution evaluation: project team or product owner.

Cultural support evaluation: OCM, HR or Super User Lead.

User maturity evaluation: Super User Lead and Super Users.

Collating and obtaining all of the above results: Super User Lead and Super Users.

Reporting on above evaluation findings to sponsor: training or Super User Lead.

Making recommendations and an action plan to address evaluation results: training or Super User Lead.

Executing and owning actions to improve adoption based on evaluation findings: project sponsor, department heads, Super Users.

16 HOW DO WE DEPLOY SUPER USERS THROUGHOUT THE SOFTWARE LIFE CYCLE?

Why Super Users should continue to be involved in your software application once it is live, and the value they can add at this stage.

PROCESS IMPROVEMENTS, PROCESS RE-ENGINEERING AND PROBLEM SOLVING

Super Users should continue to be given a portion of their time to spend on making things better for users, and for the business. Remember to approach it as if you were starting from fresh with the system you have now: what would your team structure look like and what processes would work best to get things done. What new processes are needed with the new technology? This will need incremental changes, but Super Users know your system, they know the business and they know the users. Give them the responsibility, tools and permissions to consider how we can re-engineer our processes to make work flow better between people, departments or in the system. Give them process improvement training, and the tools to map their processes, solve problems and enhance flow.

Support them not only with the training, but if it's required, help them make things happen in the system to enable their required changes to take place. It might require development, or it may just be configuration or layout changes. Plan this carefully; I would say you would not want to be doing this any more often than every three months.

ENHANCEMENTS

Enhancements may be needed as a result of the above process re-engineering, from ideation, because a feature was not in scope for the original project, or it may have been initiated by the project team to solve a particular problem. Keep your Super Users involved: they need to be informed of new features so they can consider if training is required, if training materials need updating, how the enhancement is communicated, and to perform user acceptance testing. Make the roadmap and future developments visible and transparent for Super Users during community calls.

Celebrate and promote your enhancements too; it shows our ethos of continually improving the business and the software. It also provides a vehicle for the Super Users to prove the value they add long after Go Live.

Always promote your enhancement or new feature using positive language. For example, it may be in response to an issue or error, but instead of saying 'we have fixed', frame it to users as 'you can now...' and show how they can now perform that particular task with improved speed, for example.

As always, plan your updates carefully, test them carefully, but implement them with maximum impact. Are there are any other quick wins you can deliver at the same time as the feature? Can you plan your new functionality to be done at the same time as any maintenance windows? Does it allow us to redesign a process that the new feature now enables?

Encouraging ideation and change requests for the software also helps with change acceptance and user adoption, as users can see we are committed to this system and to always making it better. Give users a portal for ideas, or filter these through Super Users for triage, assessment and prioritisation during Super User community calls. Perhaps the most upvoted idea should get a reward, to both advertise the ideation pipeline and to encourage your workforce to have that continuous improvement mindset.

UPGRADES

These may be initiated by your company as a fix, or it may be forced upon you by your software provider. An upgrade should be managed by your IT or product ownership teams, but keep your Super Users involved. They should do both user acceptance testing and regression testing to ensure there is no impact to operations. Even if you think it is a small upgrade with minor impact, make sure Super Users know it is happening. If there are any issues after deployment, then it is likely that the first to hear about them will be the Super Users, so they should not be blind that this was happening and should know exactly who to contact. Super Users can also be helpful to advise when it is best to do the upgrade, to have minimal impact during any critical or high workload periods.

BUSINESS CONTINUITY AND DISASTER RECOVERY PLANNING

It would be useful to involve Super Users in any disaster or data recovery rehearsals that your IT department should be doing. They also need to know of any business continuity plans: what happens if the system stops working for an extended period – does this mean a paper process kicks in to enable warehouses to pick customer orders? Does it mean departments may have to do manual processes that are usually automated? Does it mean we revert to a backup or legacy system? Super Users need to know all this to be sure of their role in it, and to show calm leadership in case of any adverse events, to make sure the business purpose is still fulfilled and that colleagues know how it is being resolved.

CHANGE CONTROL

You should have a robust change control procedure to ensure no changes are made to software or processes without assessment, approval and planning. Your Super Users should be a step in your change control process to assess the impact of the change request and consider what next steps are required. They will need to coordinate if any system activity must be stopped to allow the change to take place, as well as plan any comms or training updates. Make sure the changes are documented, tested and aligned with your overall strategy and objectives. You may assign the work to the most relevant

Super User for the business area, but do keep all Super Users informed too; you do not want this happening in silos as changes may have an impact on other departments. It needs to be discussed and agreed with both the product owners and the Super User community.

RETIREMENT/DECOMMISSION

As part of your software life cycle, although hopefully a long way off, your system may eventually be decommissioned. We'll use our Super Users one last time to have them assess the impact of this: what data do we need to retain for future access? What essential functions does a new system need to do? How should this change be communicated? We know we said the Super Users stay for the life of the system, but if you are replacing it with a new system, shall we start again? See you at Chapter 1.

PART III
THE THEORY SUPPORTING SUPER USER NETWORKS
'The Rationale'

- Apply organisational change management principles to the software project and Super User Model to ensure successful implementation and adoption of the technology.

- Utilise theories in neuroscience to optimise training methods, resulting in improved retention and application of knowledge.

- Transfer key principles of andragogy theories to your training and change management methodology to meet the needs of adult learners.

- Determine a knowledge management framework to support ongoing system and process competency, implementing strategies for capturing, storing and sharing knowledge.

- Analyse documented examples of project failure to apply lessons learned to your own software projects, resulting in improved project performance and reduced risk of failure.

- Differentiate between different leadership theories to influence project sponsor behaviour when leading software projects, resulting in improved project outcomes, morale and project team engagement.

17 HOW CAN CHANGE MANAGEMENT THEORY SUPPORT THE SUPER USER MODEL?

A deeper look into some theories of organisational change management, and which models are recommended for software projects.

ELEVEN STEP SUPER USER CHANGE MODEL

This simple to use 11 step framework encapsulates and summarises how Super Users are vital for change management, education and adoption (Table 17.1). This model adds to the compelling case that Super Users play an important part from the project conception through to business as usual. Following this as a framework will supercharge your digital transformation adoption.

Table 17.1 Eleven Step Super User Change Model

E	EVANGELISE	1. **Evangelise** the vision to stakeholders and Super Users using the project sponsor.
		2. **Evangelise** the benefits and case for change to end users and the overall organisation using the Super Users and communications team.
L	LISTEN	3. **Listen** to your audience on their response to the change and their preferences for training and communication.
		4. **Listen** to Super Users for advice on the system design, business process design and for user requirements.
E	EDUCATE	5. **Educate** Super Users on change management, advanced system knowledge, training skills and project-related best practice.
		6. **Educate** your end users via best practice training methods and Super User guidance.
V	VALIDATE	7. **Validate** Go Live results by tracking benefits realisation and gathering evaluation data.
E	EXECUTE	8. **Execute** actions required to improve process adoption, system capability and user ability based on evaluation data.
N	NURTURE	9. **Nurture** software with ideation, defect resolution, enhancements and improvements.

(Continued)

Table 17.1 (Continued)

10. **Nurture** the organisation through process re-engineering and organisational design to fit the future of work with your new technology.
11. **Nurture** Super Users by empowering them to instil best practice and initiate process improvements, provide them with continuous training and offer career development opportunities.

KOTTER'S CHANGE MODEL

There are many other change models that can be applied to business projects, but the '8 steps for leading change' by Dr John Kotter is one that I think applies well to system projects. Kotter's theory is good for systems as it gets people involved and our Super Users make up that brilliant volunteer army, key to your success.

1. Create a sense of urgency

Here we create our compelling case for change, with the inspirational and influential lead from our project sponsor. At a case for change workshop, we can articulate the issues with the current processes, what happens if we do nothing and what the future can be like post-implementation.

2. Build a guiding coalition

Here we build our project team of experts, perhaps outside consultants, and begin thinking about who are our 'best of the best' people for project and Super User positions.

3. Form a strategic vision and initiatives

This is our planning stage for our training and change plan, which needs to be signed off by our project sponsor. But we also need to work with our comms team on the different ways they can tell the story to the executives, to management and to end users and how we use this strategic vision to recruit our Super Users.

4. Enlist a volunteer army

Kotter's theory backs up what I have been saying all along on how using Super Users is essential for change. And they are not just there to deliver a training session; that army is our front line in keeping our end users engaged and moving along the change curve towards that strategic vision.

5. Enable action by removing barriers

This is the part where our Super Users can be involved in our business process design. They know the obstacles and inefficiencies currently, and if we can address those in the system design stage it gives us a great story to tell to our end users. We are also removing barriers to progress by creating that cross-functional team with our army of Super Users bringing their individual expertise to the table, working on that common goal for the organisation.

6. Generate short-term wins

This is where we can recognise the efforts of our Super Users throughout the process: the design we all agreed on; the swift defect resolution; the feedback from a training session. We celebrate and advertise those results at each stage to continue enthusing both that community and the project team.

7. Sustain acceleration

Oh, it is a tough, demanding time on a systems implementation project. We need great leaders to keep us motivated throughout the length of our project and the many hours we will put in, above and beyond the 'norm'. When we have had that success of Go Live, we celebrate, but we do not stop. We drive change after change using our credibility and systems expertise until we can prove the benefits realisation and see that strategic vision happen. Our project team can then move on to the next digital transformation project, but do our Super Users? No, they stay with the system and sustain that acceleration.

8. Institute change

We need to be cementing our change at this point, articulating how our new process design, new system and new behaviours are enabling future business progress and success. Your employees need to hear this from their leaders and from the comms team, but as well this shows why the Super Users need to remain in place. Your Super Users will continue to be the evangelists of this new world; they will continue to seek out opportunities for collaboration and continuous improvements. If they remain in place, and they are empowered to do what they feel is best, then they are your evidence forever of how your business can successfully institute change.

MCKINSEY 7-S MODEL

Another one that works well with digital change projects is the McKinsey 7-S Model. The framework stipulates that you consider the following categories for your project. This could be a good planning activity with your sponsor, change and project teams.

1. **Strategy:** Ensure the strategy of the system and project aligns with the company mission, vision and goals.
2. **Structure:** Consider the organisational design required to support the new ways of working your system can bring.
3. **Systems:** Do our infrastructure, processes and procedures need to be altered in order to embed the change?
4. **Shared values:** Do we have the right culture and communities in place? Here is where we can use our Super Users to evangelise how the new system can support

our values, how we interact with each other and how we get things done. Be an advocate for the new ways of working.

5. **Skills:** What skills do we need to develop in our users to support the change? The Super User Model means we use our 'best of the best' Super Users not only as change advocates, but as skilled technical people who can expertly train our teams.

6. **Style:** This category encourages us to look at the behaviours of our people. Like we did in our LNA, we can consider: what are the desired behaviours after the change project? What behaviours do we need to unlearn? How can we use Super Users to emulate the model team?

7. **Staff:** What development opportunities are there for our Super Users? What skill gaps remain in our user population? Do we need to hire, upskill or retrain anyone once we have transitioned to adopting the new technology?

KURT LEWIN'S MODEL

I find Lewin's three step change model a little too simplistic to give us enough of a framework to emulate, but it would work well for a smaller project team leading such a change, or for smaller projects like agile product development releasing regular features.

It does, however, support how the Super User role can be used for so much more than training, and how the role should remain 'on call', as a medium for adopting successful change.

1. **Unfreezing:** The need for new software or perhaps an enhancement indicates we need to unfreeze from our current state. So, we educate the organisation about the upcoming change and use our Super Users as conduits for communications. All the preparation for the change including testing and writing training materials would happen here.

2. **Changing:** Here we would train our users, and put the new system or feature live. Our Super Users should be on hand to help people become fully immersed in the new technology – there should be a big focus and push to adopt the new system during this phase.

3. **Re-freezing:** The new system is live, so we evaluate in the same way as covered in Chapter 15. If we are happy, the organisation 'freezes' and the change becomes business as usual. If evaluation indicates there is more to be done to aid adoption, the cycle will begin again with planning for how we 'unfreeze' and get people to accept the change, adapt our system to suit or receive more training. This is why Super Users need to remain in place, especially in environments where there could be a pipeline of software releases, or a continuous improvement culture instigating process improvements.

Final thoughts:

The Eleven Step Super User Change Model is the primary one to follow as it was written especially for this purpose, using Super User networks to introduce and adopt new software into an organisation.

Kotter's leading change model is an excellent one to cite to your project sponsor when making the business case for why we need our army of volunteers. Having a framework to follow for instigating change should be business as usual for any organisation that wants to stay relevant and successful; it shouldn't be debated. Dr John Kotter himself stated, 'The rate of change is not going to slow down anytime soon. If anything, competition in most industries will probably speed up even more in the next few decades.'[5]

The McKinsey 7-S Model is a great planning exercise to do at the project initiation stage with the sponsor, HR and organisational design to give us ideas for a recommended change strategy.

Lewin's change model is best suited for less complex products with regular agile releases, and so may be suitable after your initial project has gone live to manage future enhancements.

They can all play a part in enhancing technology adoption, but without any change management strategy at all, you are increasing the risk of project failure (see Chapter 21). 'More change-adept organisations report 117% increased likelihood of successful delivery of new projects than organisations that are less adept at change.'[6]

5   TopRight Leadership (2022) *20 transformational quotes on change management*. TopRight Partners. https://www.toprightpartners.com/insights/20-transformational-quotes-on-change-management/

6   Rittenhouse, J. (2014) *Change Management as a Project: Building a PMO*. Project Management Institute.

18 HOW CAN NEUROSCIENCE THEORY SUPPORT THE SUPER USER MODEL?

A high-level overview of how the latest thinking on neuroscience supports the recommended training and change management strategy.

The recommendations in this book have come from my experiences, and learning from the incredible people I have worked with in my career. But they have also come from researching my craft and spending time on professional development. Reading about how the brain functions and learns is a fascinating subject; it has influenced techniques I have tried and included in this book, and it has also pleasingly reinforced my ideas and given me the evidence as to why they work.

We will briefly explore my interpretations of the neuroscience involved, at a simplistic level, and how it has been applied to the Super User Model (Table 18.1).

Table 18.1 Neuroscience theory applied to Super User networks

The science	The application
Neural pathways are the connections that form between the neurons in our brains, creating patterns. The more we repeat a task, the stronger and more established the neural pathway becomes. This explains why a task such as making a cup of tea, or driving a familiar route, requires little conscious effort to complete.	• Repeat the process in the training sessions, with demonstrations and practice. • Provide opportunities for the task to be practised – with exercises, drop-in sessions and training aids for on-the-job support. • Provide refresher training at regular intervals. • Your training materials and session delivery should be consistent with the correct way of working, so there is one agreed way of executing a system process, rather than multiple options by preference.
Mirror neurons facilitate both the imitation-learning of actions and the simulation of other people's behaviour.	• Use Super Users to act as role models, demonstrating the best way to do things for end users to imitate and emulate.
Ongoing or acute stress can negatively impact the brain's ability to form memories and store information.	• Use change management techniques to ensure learners feel supported not pressured. • Ensure any training and elearning built is relevant, intellectually stimulating and challenging, but within the context of the role.

(Continued)

Table 18.1 (Continued)

The science	The application
However, mild stress in short doses can increase memory consolidation in the hippocampus and amygdala by inducing the brain to focus.	• Don't make the training too hard until the learner has had repeated practice and guidance. • Use 'See It; Try It; Do It' to form the basis of blended learning as we need to provide guidance, not challenge, until the learner has enough experience to provide themselves with internal guidance.
Our amygdala contains our emotional responses to threats and fear. It can trigger us to avoid certain situations that our brain perceives as a threat to us, apparent by the experiencing of stress or anxiety around a subject.	• Seek out reasons for change resistance and deploy reassuring mitigation measures or messaging. • In our learning design, we never set a user up to fail, such as by including trick questions or interactions that are too difficult to solve from the information they currently have. • We provide supportive content to enable them to build upon their learning to solve the challenges, and gamified interactions to reinforce what they have consumed.
Working memory refers to the cognitive ability to temporarily retain and manipulate information for short periods, typically lasting up to 20 minutes. It has a limited capacity, allowing us to hold only 5–9 pieces of new information at a time, depending on the complexity of the information.	• This is why we do not present too much information at once (cognitive overload). • We introduce concepts one chunk at a time, and use repetition, summarisation and reinforcement to enable the brain to move it from short-term memory to long-term memory. • We provide knowledge checks or quizzes to cement the knowledge as a memory.
The hippocampus of our brain uses episodic memory. It enables us to remember, modify and update our information from a real-world environment and social interactions.	• Use discussions to elaborate on concepts and enable the learner to form their own thoughts and insights on the subject. • In your training provide contextual role-based scenarios, use storytelling and analogies so that learners can make those connections to what it means to them and are more likely to engage with and retain the information.
The spacing effect refers to the evidence that we are better able to recall information and concepts if we learn them in multiple, spread-out sessions rather than in a single block of time.	• Always provide learners with an overview session first to see a system demonstration (**See It**) then follow up with a more practical session at a later date (**Try It; Do It**) (see Chapter 12). • Do not try to put all information a learner needs into one training session.

(Continued)

Table 18.1 (Continued)

The science	The application
	• Consider running a full day course from lunchtime till lunchtime the next day, so the brain has a sleep in between, which aids retention.
	• No one has ever listened to me before when I've suggested a nap after a training course, but one day the powers that be may let me have my napping room.
The occipital lobe in our brain makes sense of what we see. The temporal lobe processes what we hear, and the frontal lobe helps us to reason, plan and focus.	• Use a blended learning programme, with differing material, so the brain absorbs the information in multiple ways. Also referred to as Whole Brain Learning. • Vary the activities in a course so the brain has a chance to refocus, assimilate information and use different parts of its processing ability.
The medial prefrontal cortex is known to be involved in social cognition, and is activated when new material is learned in a social context.	• We have Super Users designing end user session plans together as a group, to give the social learning factor as well as have them feeling invested in the success of the project. • This is why we also set up regular community calls so Super Users are learning from each other and creating a bonded community of like-minded individuals with a common goal.
The reticular activating system is a network of neurons that manages the millions of pieces of information our brain receives at once, filters out the unnecessary items and brings anything important to our attention. This is like when you buy a yellow car thinking it is unusual, then all of a sudden you notice yellow cars everywhere as the brain now deems it relevant enough to bring it to your attention.	• Super Users drip feed additional content to end users, to keep adding to their knowledge and adding relevance. • We can also use peripheral learning in our classroom with processes or messages on our walls; we can use posters and merchandise to show system tips or ways of working reminders. • We need a continuous campaign of comms and news about our project to keep it in the minds of our learners.

(Continued)

Table 18.1 (Continued)

The science	The application
Metacognition refers to the ability to reflect on and monitor one's own thinking processes, which can enhance learning and problem-solving skills, often referred to as thinking about thinking.	• Our Super Users are going to converse with our end users in their courses, and in the workplace, to help them to understand what they already know and what they don't know, what their perceptions are about what they have learned so far and how it applies to their role. • We'll also encourage reflection after their courses for learners to make their own connections between new ideas and their existing knowledge. • We'll ask Super Users to feed back to us what further training or development they need, and have them thinking about their own learning.
The dorsal attention network in our brain is active when we are focusing on something, but uses a lot of energy. The ventral attention network manages our distractions and new information coming to our senses; this is less energy consuming and why we can be prone to distractions, as a way of conserving energy.	• To start with, we are not going to overwhelm the focused part of the brain with overly lengthy periods of concentration. We are going to provide breaks, small chunks of learning at a time and varying activities so this part of the brain naturally gets opportunities to rest before we ask it again to refocus. • It is also why we want to be engaging trainers in our virtual classrooms: try to use video for both the host and the participant and vary what the learners see by switching from our face to our demos, slides and any interactions. We want to be the ones providing that visual variation, so the distractions are not coming from people reacting to new email or phone messages.
Research in neuroscience tells us it is more effective to focus on positive messaging, i.e. what you do want, rather than what you don't.	• This is everything in how we speak to ourselves: the brain believes what we tell it; the more we reinforce positive messages to ourselves, the more we believe them and the better we feel about ourselves. • Not only is this the type of personal development we could give to our Super Users to increase their confidence, but it should also influence the messages we give in our training courses. It shouldn't be 'Don't do this because...' It should be 'The most effective way to achieve this is...' so that the brain perceives the instruction as a positive instruction, not a reprimand.

(Continued)

Table 18.1 (Continued)

The science	The application
Dopamine is a neurotransmitter that regulates our brain's response to reward stimuli.	• We need our brains to associate doing our jobs well on the system as a satisfying task, so provide praise and continual recognition to both end users and Super Users, and this should continue the motivation for doing the task in the future.
	• But actual rewards work well too – that could be prizes in a classroom quiz, a leaderboard of the course participants, getting high ratings in our performance management objectives relating to system use or even bonuses and incentives for our Super Users.
High-performing teams are a result of people acting because they choose to, not because they feel they have to. Self-directed decision making encourages employees to thrive. Having autonomy creates an environment where people are immersed in their work, can sustain focus on it and bring their skills and motivation to a task.	• HR should use this as impetus to improving employee experience for all and creating a great place to work. • But we can use this to justify why we give Super Users the autonomy to initiate process improvement ideas of their own, to have a say in the software or learning design and to feel like their thoughts and contributions are valued.

19 HOW CAN ADULT LEARNING THEORY SUPPORT THE SUPER USER MODEL?

How established adult learning theories support the recommended training and change management strategy.

I have always loved learning, but I have never liked being told what to do, and I have never liked learning information I felt I would never need. It turns out I am not that different in those feelings; adults need to be able to make the links between why they are learning and how they will apply the learning. This is why we get Super Users heavily involved in learning design, to make the case for change to end users, articulate the real-life context for the knowledge and deliver the training in an engaging way.

MALCOLM KNOWLES 4 PRINCIPLES OF ANDRAGOGY (TEACHING ADULTS)

1. **Adults prefer to have a say in how their training is organised and presented.**

   - Ensure Super Users are involved in the learning design.

   - Always explain the 'why' behind what is being trained.

   - Consult with users on training and communication preferences during a case for change session.

2. **Adults need to bring their own experiences to the table in order to gain a better understanding of the material.**

   - Apply storytelling, analogies and contextual elements to your training – it is not just about a sequential process of pressing buttons.

   - Use Super Users who can utilise their own experience of the process to better design what the software and training should look like for the 'To-Be' state.

3. **Rather than memorising facts, adults need to be able to work out problems and use their critical thinking skills in order to absorb the information.**

   - Provide blended learning opportunities for the new system including system simulations or training environments.

   - Remember the 'See It; Try It; Do It' mantra from the train the trainer course in Chapter 12.

4. **Adults need to be able to apply the knowledge to their own lives, and use it right away.**

   - Provide opportunities for the learner to practise afterwards with training system access or drop-in practice rooms.

- Ensure training support is available and easily accessible after launch to provide instruction at the point of use.

- Continually deliver training and coaching via Super Users after the launch.

JACK MEZIROW TRANSFORMATIONAL LEARNING THEORY

This theory underscores the importance of supporting learners with change management as well as with knowledge. The theory aims to transform a learner's existing frame of reference through self-reflection, tasks and problem solving. This can be facilitated through various activities, such as group discussions, role-playing and experiential learning.

Mezirow describes transformative learning as 'learning that transforms problematic frames of reference to make them more inclusive, discriminating, reflective, open, and emotionally able to change.'[7]

This is why we use Super Users in a change management capacity as well as with system training. This theory demonstrates why we provide a blended learning programme of contextual, engaging and practice based training delivered by Super Users who can facilitate discussion as well as impart expertise. We need to give the learner the frame of reference, but allow them to create their own internal narrative for what it means to them, and to their role.

DAVID KOLB EXPERIENTIAL LEARNING THEORY

Based on human psychology this encourages a more hands-on approach to adult learning and is especially relevant to software training, stipulating that adults learn best by doing.

- **Self-reflection**
  - Start off your training with a discussion, articulate the 'why' and encourage end users to approach Super Users with questions after reflection.
- **Active involvement**
  - Involve Super Users in learning design and ensure end users receive training from these experts in their own area.
- **Conceptualising the experience**
  - Again, add real-life context to system training. You are executing a business function for a reason, not just pressing buttons.
- **Using the knowledge learned from it in real life**
  - Deliver training close to launch, during hypercare and on an ongoing basis.

---

7   Mezirow, J. (2009) Transformative learning theory. In: Mezirow, J. and Taylor, E.W. (eds). *Transformative Learning in Practise: Insights from Community*. Jossey-Bass

- ○ Super Users can provide either coaching or training materials to ensure the user is supported at the point of use.
- ○ Learning the system is just as important during this 'Do It' part of 'See It; Try It; Do It' as it's only when you are using the training for real, that the capability comes to be embedded as habit.

MCCALL, LOMBARDO AND EICHINGER 70:20:10 MODEL

This model suggested that 70% of training is on the job, 20% from peers, and only 10% from formal traditional training. Consider the list below when designing your blended learning curriculum with your Super Users.

Experiential 70%

- scenario-based contextual learning;
- system simulations or training environments;
- at the point of use training aids or guides;
- practical on-the-job training by a Super User.

Social 20%

- Super User coaching and demonstrating best practice;
- user communities;
- social learning groups;
- interactive webinars.

Formal 10%

- onboarding courses;
- instructor-led training;
- elearning courses;
- knowledge management resources.

KENNETH NOWACK 55:25:20 MODEL

Revised from the above, this model may be a better fit for system adoption and employee retention.

Experiential 55%

- my 'See It; Try It; Do It' training strategy from Chapter 12.

Social 25%

- keeping Super Users acting as a community;

- giving Super Users the accountability to instil product adoption, best practices and process improvement in their own teams;

- encouraging a culture of personal and professional development that colleagues share with each other;

- knowledge management tools that enable discussion, comments and collaboration (see next chapter).

Formal 20%

- onboarding new colleagues;

- continually providing training to Super Users and in turn to end users;

- formal certification in the software, if this exists.

Final thoughts...

From the theories we have discovered in this chapter, we know that adults need to know why they are learning something, and how it applies to their role. This is why change management is so important to software projects so that this is stated explicitly through communications and through reiterating it in training sessions.

But it also shows how adults need practical support for learning. They need to be able to put the learning to use as quickly as possible. This is why we cannot learn new software from a sole source such as a video, an elearning course or from instructional documents. They are all useful training methods that we should use to provide support, but it does not compare to having a training system, or simulation, that users can practise on. We must insist on this to deliver effective software training.

20 HOW CAN KNOWLEDGE MANAGEMENT THEORY SUPPORT THE SUPER USER MODEL?

Considerations for a knowledge management strategy to support Super User networks.

We need a knowledge management strategy to ensure that knowledge can be shared by those who have it, and accessed by those who need it. This should be part of the culture of your organisation. In this chapter, we will touch on why this is important and the factors you should consider.

WHY DO WE NEED A KNOWLEDGE MANAGEMENT STRATEGY?

Yes, we have Super Users who will play a vital part, but we still need to ensure people can access the information they need without having to wait for a Super User response. Super Users can be great enablers for a good knowledge management strategy, but they are only part of it. When we have a knowledge management strategy, our end users don't have to remember everything we teach them, they just need to remember where to find the information when they need it.

Here are the reasons we need a complete strategy:

- a culture of personal growth;
- accessing company data for analytical purposes;
- best practice standards;
- day-to-day employee tasks;
- troubleshooting and resolving queries;
- onboarding new employees or community members;
- retaining information from leavers and retirees;
- self-serve customer service;
- to assist with mergers and acquisitions.

TYPES OF KNOWLEDGE MANAGEMENT

1. **Knowledge creation:** We need Super Users to ensure training material is created for both systems and process knowledge. You can also consider, if you have the function available, enabling **any** user to create 'How-To' guides. If you wish to do

this, I would recommend you have a review step to ensure Super Users regularly check the user-generated content for accuracy and best practice.

2. **Knowledge storage:** We need a common place where information can be accessed. Ideally, we want it to be the same place where users go to access any knowledge, and not just our system. But we can do either, as long as it is:

   • branded for easy identification of our system information (optional but recommended);

   • easy to access at the point of use;

   • easy to save favourites or collections;

   • intuitive to search and find relevant information quickly;

   • widely communicated to intended users.

3. **Knowledge sharing:** Super Users do this as part of their community calls, but can also play a part in making sure people are pointed to the right material in response to questions or requests. A comments section works really well so users can add their thoughts, questions and amendment ideas, but also, a user's name can be tagged to bring their attention to the article they need. Make sure your chosen IT technology has the function to share a link directly to the chosen content.

4. **Knowledge maintenance:** It should be a Super User responsibility to ensure any documentation or training material is reviewed regularly and kept accurate – with a mechanism for easily sharing or identifying if it has been recently updated. It is important therefore for your product owners or centre of excellence (CoE) to keep Super Users abreast of changes, and that Super Users can continue to devote a portion of their day-to-day role to Super User responsibilities.

METHODS OF KNOWLEDGE MANAGEMENT

• **AI chat bot**

There are some great tools you can use now to incorporate AI or natural language processing into your chat bots. Please do make sure a customer can connect with a human when they need to though. AI and automation provide essential services for organisational efficiency and knowledge transfer, but they should never replace valuable human-to-human connection.

• **Bespoke system**

Build your own knowledge management space in accordance with your requirements, aimed at differing functions or roles, perhaps incorporating all we recommend here. (Do you need Super Users for that?)

• **Big data, dashboards, data visualisation**

We need easy access to the organisation's information and it needs to be visually clear to enable informed, speedy decision making. Unless it is sensitive or confidential, please do not restrict access to your data and dashboards. Let all colleagues see what management can see. Consider how quickly it can speed up and encourage problem solving and process improvement initiatives if our people can simply see data on recent complaints, order trends or quality incidents. Don't put barriers in the way of your knowledge.

- **Chat tool:** Teams/Slack/RingCentral/Google Chat/Hangouts and so on.

  Perfect for collaborating with instant messaging, team relationships, meeting notes and remote teams. This should play just one part in your knowledge management strategy though.

- **Collaboration software**: Confluence, Asana, Basecamp, Monday, Notion and others

  Easy to use, good for knowledge articles, allows collaboration, sharing and comments.

- **Community threads**

  A community space to ask questions or post ideas, where other users can reply to the threads with answers or their own thoughts. It is a great tool, but one I would combine with a place to easily access published procedures, articles or guides.

- **Content management system**

  Like a document management system but for other media, ordinarily intended for websites and applications. Again, I wouldn't lock this down if licences are not an issue; these are still a valuable part of knowledge sharing. Let all of your colleagues have access to branded graphics, stock photos or other assets. Or make sure these are available on an intranet or other location.

- **Data warehouse**

  Although not likely to be accessed by our end users, it is still a vital part in a knowledge management strategy. You want all of your data, static and transactional, to be stored in a central data warehouse. This enables an accurate single source of the truth to be able to be integrated easily with other systems, reporting tools or dashboards.

- **Document management system**

  Good to use as a centralised storage system of knowledge, with version control, approvals and workflows. Consider how you can categorise your knowledge into specific buckets and make it easily searchable for what an end user needs at the point of use.

- **Expert directory**

  A directory of employees, that includes your Super Users, with specialised knowledge or skills so you can find the right person to ask for help or advice.

- **FAQs**

  A simple list of the most frequently asked questions. It is great to have at the introduction of new technology, but it is not enough for a knowledge management strategy.

- **Google Workspace/Office 365**

  Great for collaborating and easy to access and use. I might be more inclined to recommend this as part of a knowledge creation strategy, but not for storage or accessing published final versions.

- **Help portal**

  Include FAQs, a knowledge base of articles and ticketing, and ensure it is all easily searchable with an intuitive interface.

- **Intranet**

  Essentially a website or cloud sharing tool, but just for internal use. You can do all sorts with an intranet; just make sure you communicate it properly so people know what is in there and how to access it.

- **Learning management system**

  This system can administer your classroom courses and distribute your digital content. Great for onboarding and skills development; for knowledge management it will depend on whether users can quickly and easily get to the answers they need and then continue doing their task.

- **Lotus Notes**

  I might have just kept this one in here to amuse me. I'm sure it was 40 years old already when I first started using it. It served a useful purpose for a time though didn't it?

- **Metaverse**

  I haven't used this yet for a learning experience; I may be a laggard on the adoption curve. But I know it's coming. Our avatars will be there in an immersive virtual environment accessing information in a library, collaborating with others, attending training courses, meeting others to access their information and creating content for sharing. As the technology continues to evolve, it is likely that we will see more organisations adopting the metaverse for learning and knowledge management purposes.

- **SharePoint**

  An easy way of storing information with version control, and collaboration and sharing features. But you don't have to use it just for document folders, you can create great intranet pages to store documents, advertise events, share news, forms, organisation charts and more.

- **Social network:** For example Yammer or Workplace

  A social network site for just your organisation. Valuable for communities such as our Super Users, but also for end users too. We can post news, ask questions and access pinned posts or files. A great tool for social learning groups to continue to collaborate and grow after training courses too.

- **SOPs**

  Standard operating procedures are step-by-step instructions for executing a process or task in the desired or compliant way. Consider how you will review, update and handle version control – as well as ensuring people are working to the most recent edition. Valuable and clear as these are, I would consider more collaborative ways of sharing information in addition to this.

- **Wikis**

  A good tool or model to emulate, if we are going to allow creation of guides, for example, by anyone. But because anyone can create and edit a wiki, it will need an owner or a regular Super User task to ensure the relevant wikis for our system remain accurate.

COMMUNITIES OF PRACTICE THEORY

'Communities of practice' is a model described by Lave and Wenger in 1991 that reinforces the Super User Model, as it articulates that knowledge is shared under the optimal conditions that include a group of common interests, social interaction and trust.

This is why we want our Super User in the first place to be a credible, influential person among their peers, so the information that is passed on is trusted and more likely to be embedded. It is also why we do not want Super Users operating in silos; we want them uplifting each other as a community by continually examining what the best practice should be, what they have learned, what they can pass on to each other and how this knowledge can be disseminated among others to raise standards or solve issues.

I can't take any credit for it, as it just evolved naturally. But I once observed a group of field engineers who worked with complex plant machinery. They had manuals and user guides, 'How-To' videos, manufacturer support contracts and ticketing systems – a beyond reproach knowledge management strategy – but they still regularly came across new and unique problems they had no instructions for how to resolve. The majority of the time they solved them still; I can't say how, these were very skilled engineers. But once a month they got together, outside work, and socialised and swapped these stories, as anecdotes of how they overcame the challenge. It meant they were all continually learning from each other and retaining that 'how-to' knowledge through storytelling, by operating as a community of practice. And a very British habit: they did all this from the pub.

SINGLE AND DOUBLE LOOP LEARNING THEORY

Simply put, single loop learning is where you correct a problem that has occurred. Double loop learning ensures you look at the cause and potential improvements to prevent the issue occurring again, and document this new step or change in your knowledge management resources. If you think back to what I said at the start of the chapter, we need knowledge to be shared by those who have it, and accessed by those who need it. That is single loop learning; it's about getting existing knowledge to solve the immediate issue. But when we empower our Super Users to continue to operate in a world where they are empowered to challenge that existing knowledge, to look at what can be improved, to build and create new knowledge, we are creating the conditions that enable double loop learning.

I worked in the life sciences industry where corrective and preventive actions (CAPAs) were regulated and had to be completed and documented for compliance. This can be done on quality management systems, on spreadsheets, on paper forms – and, yes, the fact that preventive action is considered as part of every quality issue or near miss is indeed double loop learning. However, this company had a great approach to socialising the knowledge as part of a community and embedding the learning process as part of the culture.

In every business area there were dedicated rooms with whiteboards kitted out with templates to conduct problem-solving exercises. Think fishbone diagrams, root cause analysis, problem statements and failure mode effect analysis. The exercise was then never completed by one person at a desk; it was conducted as a team event (which often included the system Super User for the area) so that the example of double loop learning became knowledge that was shared and communicated widely. Everywhere you went you saw these problem-solving boards being widely used, the results were included in colleague newsletters, recognition was often given publicly to the teams and this culture of embedding the practice and socialising the learning became new knowledge for all.

This is exactly the approach we want Super Users to take with problem solving: work on it together, think about how issues can be prevented, how the agreed solution can be communicated and how the acquired knowledge can become embedded as standard practice. Encourage this to be part of your culture too by empowering Super Users to keep this activity as an objective for their role.

UNLEARNING, KNOWLEDGE DILUTION AND UNKNOWNS

Unlearning

- It can be daunting and anxiety inducing to have to start from scratch to learn something new. We need to acknowledge those are valid feelings, but still articulate why the change was necessary and how end users will be supported.

- The end users now need to unlearn the previous way of doing things, which is why in our learning design we need to consider not just the button-pressing side of system training, but what desired behaviours we are wanting to see after Go Live.

- Unlearning can be an opportunity. Examine what behaviours and activities were happening before your new system. What can we do differently now? You have implemented automation software as an example, so what intellectually stimulating tasks can you give your people to do instead to add value? Do we really need people inputting data onto spreadsheets all day when we have new business intelligence dashboards? Ask your people what they can be doing with those data insights to enhance customer experience, or with that time given back. All those projects and improvements you'd never had time to do before, you might be able to pursue now.

- We need to monitor performance and results on the system for a while, to check the system is being used as trained, as old habits are hard to break. The only way to make new habits is to immerse yourself in practice, repetition and by receiving positive reinforcement – which our Super Users provide.

- Our Super Users were likely to have been in the same situation. They were already known as experts in their departments, which is why we recruited them, so it is more than likely they were experts in their old legacy software too. They had to unlearn 'the way we do things' with their old systems, but the valuable knowledge they had gave us great insight into designing our processes in the most efficient way for the new system.

Unknown unknowns

- End users don't know what they don't know. Or in more academic terms, these are unknown unknowns. We couldn't teach our end users everything before Go Live; they would never have retained all of that new information. We gave them the basics they needed to do their jobs and now we are providing training support to build on that knowledge.

- By asking Super Users to continually provide system training, we get to eliminate the unknowns and build on end user expertise. There may be other reporting we did not show them at first. Maybe there are new system integrations we can take advantage of, or other new features we have never used before that Super Users can explore to see if they can be of benefit. We won't leave end users with that same basic level of knowledge we had at Go Live – we will continue providing system tips and new improved ways of working to eliminate the unknowns.

Knowledge dilution

- It's Joe's first day at his new job. He sits next to the lovely Sandra who is asked to train him up and help him get started. Sandra shows Joe about 80% of what she knows on the system, thinking she'll just show him the remaining system transactions when he asks. It's been two years now since the system went live, but Sandra knows the system really well, although she thinks she might have forgotten some of her training. But it's fine, she is getting by OK with what she does know. Skip to another year later, and it is Amir's first day at work. He sits next to the lovely Joe who is asked to train him up and get him started. Joe feels he knows the system reasonably well but only shows Amir some of it for now, just the basics. And so it goes on when we ask the very lovely and well-meaning staff to train up the new employees. Can you see how the system expertise, process knowledge or issue resolution skills will get diluted over time?

- Contrast the above approach with the Super User Model. Our Super Users have remained system experts as they have continually received training themselves from the product owners or CoE team or software provider. They still have a high level of knowledge even two years after Go Live. They keep training material accurate to be used for onboarding, and they have responsibility for the systems training of their new colleagues. They can support them with the material, with coaching or with training sessions to ensure new colleagues all learn the same best practice skills – from the basics, to the more advanced value-added system tips.

IT'S NOT WHAT YOU KNOW

Let us finish off with that old saying, 'it's not what you know, it's who you know'. Well actually all the 'knows' are important, but we can cover them all with Super User networks.

- **Know what**

  Our end users know **what** skills, tasks and knowledge are necessary to perform in their jobs.

- **Know where**

  Our end users know **where** to access the support and tutorial information they need.

- **Know when**

  Our end users know **when** Super Users will be providing new and refresher training to enhance their knowledge.

- **Know why**

  Our end users know **why** the system was rolled out, why a process is designed that way, what impact it has or process it triggers and the benefits to the organisation, customer and employee.

- **Know how**

  Our end users know **how** to execute the processes or system tasks.

- **Know who**

  Importantly, our end users know **who** to contact for expert knowledge and advice – our Super Users.

21 HOW CAN PROJECT FAILURE RESEARCH SUPPORT THE SUPER USER MODEL?

Why digital transformation projects are not always delivered successfully and how the Super User Model can mitigate the contributing factors.

A 2001 survey across all sectors published by BCS found that only around one in eight IT projects (13%) were successful (i.e. delivered on time, to cost and to specification).[8] Forbes, McKinsey, John Kotter and others have been quoted as saying that 70% of strategic change projects fail.[9] That is because it doesn't matter what technology your digital transformation project is implementing, it's people that drive change and make things happen. To make your software projects successful, people need to adopt the technology and that means getting them engaged, involved and invested in making the change a success.

Super Users won't fix all of your problems I'm afraid, but they do give us a better chance of product adoption and project success. In Table 21.1 we can see typical reasons why projects fail. It is subjective but I have indicated 📖 for those for which this book suggests preventive strategies.

Table 21.1 Common causes of project failure

People	Process	Technology
Doing project work as well as the day job 📖	Lack of budget or funding	Building costly bespoke systems when suitable off-the-shelf products exist
Inadequate leadership 📖	Lack of communication 📖	Ignoring the technology roadmap, i.e. using soon to be obsolete software
Case for change not articulated or understood 📖	Risks not tracked and managed	Inaccurate system master data 📖
Inadequate training 📖	Lack of planning	Inadequate data management and security policies

(Continued)

---

8 Pearce, S. (2003) *Government IT Projects*. The Parliamentary Office of Science and Technology. https://www.parliament.uk/globalassets/documents/post/pr200.pdf

9 Percy, S. (2019) *Why do change programs fail?* Forbes. https://www.forbes.com/sites/sallypercy/2019/03/13/why-do-change-programs-fail/?sh=62090d32e48b

Table 21.1 (Continued)

People	Process	Technology
Too many meetings not enabling work to get done on time	Lack of project management process or expertise	Inadequate testing
Organisational culture	Benefits not tracked or realised	Inadequate time for defect resolution
Lack of resource in project team – technical and business	No change management activities	Scope creep due to additional requirements
'Red-flags' or 'No-Go' decisions ignored	Too many projects or too much change at once	Technology not fit for purpose
Change resistance not addressed		

REPORTED PROJECT FAILURES

Unfortunately, the data doesn't exist to know whether the companies shown below used Super Users in any capacity, but we can surmise that best practices in software projects were not followed, due to the reasons for project failure that have been reported (Table 21.2).

Table 21.2 Project failure examples

Who?	What happened?	What could have happened?
Apple	In the 1990s, Apple developed the Copland operating system to compete with Windows for the Mac, but the project experienced scope creep due to additional features and requirements added by different departments, leading to delayed delivery and eventual cancellation.	Prevent scope creep by involving users in the initial design and then locking down the requirements for delivery. Cover your additional requirements in future releases.
City of Portland	An enterprise resource planning (ERP) project for the City of Portland, US, saw spiralling costs and extending delivery dates due to changing internal requirements and lack of resources for training and system design.	Involve Super Users who know the business in the requirements and design stages. Educate Super Users in best practice training delivery and ensure you recruit enough of them to provide adequate resource.

(Continued)

Table 21.2 (Continued)

Who?	What happened?	What could have happened?
Dorset County Council	Dorset County Council, UK, introduced a system that the users felt was slower than their previous system and hated using. 'The overall feedback is that 58% (of users) feel negative with concerns about training, usability and support.'[10]	Super Users need to be involved in the system design as well as the training delivery. IT projects need to be done **with** the business, not **for** the business. User acceptance testing should be an integral part of the business readiness process, and the system should not Go Live if the business does not provide acceptance for the system.
FBI	FBI initiated a large project for virtual case files that had a too-short project timeline and a big bang Go Live planned that would retire the legacy system, and put the new system live all in one weekend.	With Super User resource you can plan a phased approach to delivery of the system, as minimising business disruption should be a criterion for Go Live. Use Super Users as part of a cutover rehearsal to test your system migration approach.
FoxMeyer	FoxMeyer had an unrealistic project timeline for their warehouse management system, and a workforce with unaddressed fears and resistance to change. This resulted in a costly and overrunning project, with users who had no desire to adopt the new solution to the extent there was active sabotage affecting service delivery.	Start with a realistic project plan. Getting it right is more important than getting it quick. If there is disruption to be felt from the project, this should be borne internally, and not externally by customers or shareholders. Super Users should be used to talk to and listen to end users about the reasons for their resistance to the change, and implement strategies to counteract these fears. Super Users cannot solve everything though; you need to be transparent if the new organisational design may affect job security. Value your people during this process, as not only can it put your project at risk but your

(Continued)

---

10 Snapp, S. (2020) *A list of SAP implementation failures.* Brightwork Research. https://www.brightworkresearch.com/list-of-sap-implementation-failures/

Table 21.2 (Continued)

Who?	What happened?	What could have happened?
		reputation may be forever tarnished for not doing so. Can you reskill your workers at risk? Could you provide bonus incentives to exiting employees if you need them to assist with the transition? Can you provide them with other support to minimise disruption to their careers and future?
Haribo	Haribo's ERP upgrade project did not go well because the technology build did not align to company strategy and business requirements. Lack of leadership and lack of testing were also contributing factors.	Super Users should sign off the business requirements and system or process design. Super Users should be involved in testing and have a say in any business readiness conversations.
Hershey's	Characterised again by an unrealistic project timeline, Hershey's came under pressure to Go Live at Halloween, typically their busiest time. Users had not been fully trained by this point, and were not confident or quick enough on the system yet to meet demands, resulting in supply chain disruption and missed orders.	I have seen training windows squeezed before to meet Go Live dates. You may have done well to meet all your project deliverables in a tight project timescale, but if your users do not know how to properly use your amazing system, then all that hard work was for nothing. Ensure that having trained and competent users is part of your business readiness criteria, and allow time for adoption, evaluation and to move along the learning curve before facing any peaks or seasonal demand.
Israel Chemical Ltd	This company wide ERP project was led by finance, but the manufacturing and supply chain sections of the business had not been consulted on the requirements. Employees and business managers felt the system was being forced on them and user adoption suffered.	Use Super Users and your sponsor to engage with all areas of the business for communications, stakeholder engagement and buy-in. Recruit Super Users from all business functions to ensure the requirements are a fit for all areas.

(Continued)

Table 21.2 (Continued)

Who?	What happened?	What could have happened?
LeasePlan	A large system upgrade was considered to have failed as users rejected the new system due to a lack of consideration, training and change management.	Training needs to be delivered by Super Users as those being trained are more likely to accept it when it is delivered by people they know, trust and value.
		Use your Super Users as change agents and project team members, not just trainers.
National Grid (USA)	An already overdue project was pressured to Go Live, when tests were still failing and defects had not been resolved. When they went live anyway, employees were paid incorrectly and vendor invoices couldn't be processed.	Don't just have testing as a window on your project plan; ensure time is marked out for defect resolution. Plan this accurately to know how many tests you need to run per day with what resource you have, then allow time afterwards to resolve the defects we **want** them to find.
		Listen to your Super Users and project team at Go/No-Go business readiness meetings and of course never Go Live with critical defects outstanding.
Target Canada	Data was not migrated from Target's legacy system to the new system, and instead inexperienced entry level employees entered new data into the system. This resulted in going live with only 30% of their master data being accurate, causing supply chain and financial disruption.	This is why we value the business knowledge that Super Users bring: they would have been better equipped to spot the errors in the data.
		Ensure data validation is a task in your project plan and there is no one better to provide the final sign-off that the data is correct than your Super Users.

The UK Parliamentary Office of Science and Technology conducted a study of over 100 public sector IT projects to understand why so many were deemed to have failed.

Their conclusions were:

- Rapidly changing technology.
- Difficulties in defining requirements and high complexity.
- IT projects are meant to be linked to departments' overall objectives and deliver benefits for the department.

- Breaking projects down into smaller parts increases the chances of success and makes contingency planning easier.

- It is important to include the final users in project development and provide time and resources for training.

The study concluded with 'The people who will eventually use an IT service should be involved in IT projects for three reasons. Firstly, the initial requirements should be based on users' needs and testing should accurately reflect the demands on the service. Secondly, users are involved to build ownership and reduce resistance to change. If the end users are hostile to a project, it is less likely to result in benefits for the department. Finally, the training needs of end users should be built into the project. To be most effective, training needs to take place just before the skills are to be used – this is a particular problem for large, "big bang" implementations, where training all the users could take months. As well as time and resources for training, project teams also need to recognise that staff productivity may drop immediately after implementation, while people get used to the new service.'[11]

Final thoughts...

I think you'll agree from reading that final study that Super Users could have certainly helped achieve success on those UK public sector projects, and the report's conclusions could have helped with the project failures from our other examples too.

11 Pearce, S. (2003) *Government IT Projects*. The Parliamentary Office of Science and Technology. https://www.parliament.uk/globalassets/documents/post/pr200.pdf

22 HOW CAN LEADERSHIP THEORY SUPPORT THE SUPER USER MODEL?

Expectations and requirements for senior leadership and project sponsors to demonstrate particular leadership styles to support Super User networks and software projects.

To be instigating digital transformation projects in the first place, I'd like to think this already demonstrates the forward-thinking leadership you have in your organisation. This book is not here to convince leaders on why digital transformation is necessary; there are other books for that. But we should examine leadership theory so we can set the right expectations for what we need from our C-suite level and our project sponsor to support successful implementation of a Super User network.

We need to spend time with the sponsor at the beginning of the project to gain their buy-in to using a Super User network and get their commitment to its' sustained implementation. Present an executive summary to them on the resource demands on your training team if you didn't use Super Users, and the lack of business expertise that could bring – then present the benefits mentioned in this book if you did deploy Super Users.

I recognise that the relationship is more likely to be that the sponsor chooses you to be part of the project, rather than us having the autonomy to select the sponsor – but it still helps to understand what we need from our leaders on digital transformation projects. Now, if the C-suite are undergoing any kind of executive coaching, those are the people you want to engage with to attempt to get them to influence the kind of leadership you need.

The sponsor should be the most senior manager who is directly responsible for the business function that is going through the change. For cross-functional projects, the most relevant C-suite executive should be the sponsor.

Digital transformation projects require a project sponsor that:

- provides leadership;
- inspires innovation;
- evangelises the benefits;
- supports the programme;
- removes obstacles;
- offers guidance and expertise;
- empowers the team;
- drives successful delivery.

'Good leaders create a vision, articulate the vision, passionately own the vision and relentlessly drive it to completion'.[12]

SITUATIONAL THEORY OF LEADERSHIP

The Situational Theory of Leadership by Dr Paul Hersey and Kenneth Blanchard advises that success does not depend on having one leadership style, but being able to adapt to suit the situation. This fits with software projects, as we need all these different styles in one person.

The situational theory of leadership describes these styles as:

- **Autocratic: Giving orders.** Suitable for a leadership style in combat zones or hospitals, for example when people's lives rely on the leader giving the right orders and people following them. But this would not make a good leadership style for a project that depends on people's willingness and motivation to do a good job. However, we need them to be able to use this style to demonstrate enough authority on the occasions when they have to escalate issues, remove obstacles or obtain more resources.

- **Selling: Motivating a team with little experience needs a combination of telling and selling.** Although we do train and develop our team members, they should only be in the team if they have existing software experience, project management skills or business knowledge. So, this approach doesn't quite apply. However, we do need leaders to be able to use this skill to sell the vision to the business. Without leadership selling a compelling vision and top-down mandate for the use of technology in our organisation's future, the project's success is less likely. We need them to have the skills, reputation and influence to drive and motivate the team to success while gaining business and stakeholder buy-in.

- **Participating: A democratic approach to a skilled team.** These leaders encourage participation and contributions from the team, and value their expertise in the decision-making process. But the ultimate responsibility lies with the leader still. This helps us as we need them to back us up in our decisions, while also taking ownership for the success of the project, without a blame culture. We need them to be trusting enough to rely on the expertise of the team they have selected, without micromanaging.

- **Delegating: A hands off approach.** I like these leaders: just trust me to do my job as I am confident in my ability and my judgement. We want them to lead and stay informed without getting involved in the minor details and decisions. But again, we would not want this all the time. We need them present and involved; we need them to show they are just as driven as us to get the results.

---

12 Goodreads (no date) *Jack Welch quotes*. Goodreads. https://www.goodreads.com/quotes/476679-good-business-leaders-create-a-vision-articulate-the-vision-passionately

TRANSFORMATIONAL LEADERSHIP THEORY

This theory by Bass is perfect for long projects as it proposes that a leader needs to inspire their people to achieve goals by creating a collective purpose.

- **Individualised consideration:** An empathetic leader needs to understand individuals in the team and try to guide or mentor them accordingly.

- **Intellectual stimulation:** The project sponsor should set the standard by offering the latest research and intellectual insights for the software or their industry, in order to encourage the team to do the same, pursue innovation and use intelligent decision making.

- **Inspirational motivation:** They create a team by inspiring and motivating everyone to come together to pursue a common goal.

- **Idealised influences:** The leader is seen as a role model for employees to emulate, either because of their standing in the industry or their reputation in the organisation.

SERVANT LEADERSHIP THEORY

Robert Greenleaf's servant leadership theory suggests that the project sponsor should put their primary focus on the relationship between themselves and their project team. The sponsor should aim to create a collaborative environment where trust, understanding and values are at the forefront. The goal for the leader is to serve their followers' needs first and foremost, so they in turn will work together more effectively and produce better results. The leader's dedication to the wellbeing of the group should result in increased motivation, better collaboration and, ultimately, superior performance.

I can vouch for this one on software projects: servant leaders create a great environment to work in.

Final thoughts...

Software projects are demanding – we have the expertise; it is your role as a leader to keep us feeling valued and motivated. Get to know your people, join the social events, learn the personal details, ask people how they are doing or what they need, thank them for their recent work (with specifics).

It is almost embarrassing, but I remember just how much it meant to me when the senior leaders knew my name and gave me praise. I happily worked those late nights and weekends, and pushed for the milestones, for those leaders.

PART IV
SUSTAINING THE SUPER USER NETWORK
'The Conclusion'

- Consider the different project team roles and how they should interact with Super Users to leverage their value and contribution to all aspects of the project life cycle.

- Explore the recommended software applications that Super User networks are suitable for.

- Utilise the Super User network and best practice recommendations to improve system knowledge and long-term user adoption of new technology.

- Determine methods to sustain the Super User community and their value-added role in the organisation beyond Go Live.

- Discover final recommendations and key takeaways for the compelling case to use Super User networks in software and digital transformation projects.

23 HOW WILL OTHER PROJECT ROLES WORK WITH YOUR SUPER USERS?

A framework for what interactions your Super Users should have with each project team member.

Have I mentioned before that Super Users are not just for training? Possibly once, but let us reinforce that idea by summarising how your Super Users will work with other roles during your software implementation. Whether you're working agile, waterfall projects or running a centre of excellence model, it is likely you will have a mix of people in your teams, as shown in Table 23.1.

Table 23.1 Super User and project team interactions

Project role	Interaction with Super User
Business intelligence or reporting lead	• Keep Super Users informed of any dashboards or reporting developed relating to technology use, incident management or adoption metrics
Business process owner or lead	• Spend time with Super Users to understand the 'As-Is' processes, business rules and procedures
	• Involve Super Users in deciding the 'To-Be' solution
	• Educate Super Users on each business process
	• Forge a close working relationship
Centre of excellence lead	• Work with Super Users on establishing best practice standards and a continuous improvement approach
Communications manager	• Consult with Super Users on communications plan
	• Assist Super Users with communications for training courses
	• Use Super Users to feed back attitudes and responses to the messaging used in comms campaigns
	• Highlight and promote recognition of Super Users' work and achievements
	• Ensure a pipeline of news and comms stories both to and from Super Users

(Continued)

Table 23.1 (Continued)

Project role	Interaction with Super User
Computer systems validation lead	• Educate Super Users on validation rules and regulations • Educate Super Users on data integrity and compliance where required • Request Super User assistance in completing risk assessments and validation documentation
Cutover manager	• Consult with Super Users on what tasks are required for a cutover plan • Communicate cutover task procedures and plan details to Super Users • Liaise with Super Users on completion status of cutover tasks • Provide advice and solutions to blockers or escalated issues
Data analysts	• Involve Super Users in any data validation activities • Request Super Users assist with any data collection, cleansing or mapping • Work with Super Users to test and validate data migration
Documentation manager	• Ensure Super Users are educated on good documentation practice and any compliance requirements • Provide accountability for an RTM • Assist Super Users in managing version control with approved copies signed and stored, and new versions circulated for approval
HR lead	• Ensure Super Users are considered in any talent mapping exercises, and any talent development or growth opportunities • Include Super Users in any succession planning activities as a key role for the organisation • Support managers in nurturing Super User career development • Fulfil HR requirement by backfilling roles and managing any project secondments

(Continued)

Table 23.1 (Continued)

Project role	Interaction with Super User
IT support lead	• Make sure the helpdesk support team attends system familiarisation and business process training sessions with Super Users
	• Educate Super Users on how to report issues both from themselves and on behalf of end users
	• Ensure Super Users are included as a step in the support model
	• Keep Super Users informed of critical issues and outages reported
	• Provide Super Users with requested equipment or test and training environments
L&D or education services	• Utilise Super Users in keeping training material accurate and current
	• Educate Super Users in technical tools such as screen recorders or your LMS
	• Provide mentoring and best practice advice to Super Users in generating training materials or delivering courses
Organisational change manager	• Educate Super Users on change management techniques and theories
	• Continually consult with Super Users on action plans to handle change resistance and acceptance
	• Inform Super Users in advance of any organisational design changes
Process or business analyst	• Spend time with Super Users to understand the 'As-is' processes, business rules and procedures
	• Involve Super Users in the process of business and user requirements gathering
	• Keep Super Users informed of useful documentation such as process flows and solution build specifications
Product manager	• Ensure Super Users and other roles understand the long-term future roadmap and vision for the software
	• Request Super User input on ideation for future development

(Continued)

Table 23.1 (Continued)

Project role	Interaction with Super User
Product owner	• Keep Super Users informed of enhancements and features in development and use them for testing, communications and rollout
	• Ensure Super Users are continually educated on solutions built and new features
	• Request Super User input on ideation and prioritisation for future developments
Project manager	• Involve Super Users in creating and finalising a project plan
	• Engage with Super Users on dates, changes and completion of tasks
	• Provide advice and solutions for any blockers or escalated issues
	• Give Super Users a voice at any stage-gate reviews or Go/No-Go decision meetings
Project sponsor	• Provide inspirational leadership and motivation to all your team
	• Have a physical presence at case for change and Super User onboarding sessions
	• Provide a video introduction of the project vision to show in end user training sessions or comms
	• Provide personalised thanks, rewards and recognition
Scrum Master	• Educate Super Users on agile methodologies. tools and techniques
	• Liaise with Super Users on work in progress
	• Involve Super Users in sprint planning, sprint reviews, scrums and retrospectives
Security and role consultants	• Involve Super Users in end user role, access and permissions mapping
	• Ensure Super Users are included as an approval step to verify training completion for new user access requests
	• Ensure auditing, security and data integrity procedures exist if Super Users have additional system access.

(Continued)

Table 23.1 (Continued)

Project role	Interaction with Super User
Solutions developer or consultant	• Understand the user requirements as established by Super Users and other roles • Ensure Super Users understand the technical solution (possibly via the business process owner) • Work with Super Users on providing defect fixes that meet business and user requirements
Super User Lead	• Deploy as much of the best practice advice in this book as possible • Get copies of this book for your Super Users or your library • Recommend this book to others
Test analyst or manager	• Attend system familiarisation and business process training sessions with Super Users • Work with Super Users on establishing the test cases required and data set needed • Collaborate with Super Users on writing or approving the test scripts • Agree who is running which test scripts • Report on test completion, defects and critical path analysis to complete testing on time • Advise Super Users of test defects categorised as business process, data issue, user error or system solution required • Involve Super Users in resolving and retesting defects • Liaise with Super Users on who will complete UAT (can be business users or Super Users, see Chapter 4)
UX developer or analyst	• Solicit feedback from Super Users on the user interface before design is final (preferably when an MVP version)

24 WHAT SYSTEMS CAN I USE SUPER USERS WITH?

A list of digital platforms suitable for using a Super User network.

In my first job, I wrote a business case to justify why we should purchase Microsoft Word instead of using typewriters or handwriting our faxes. That gives you an indication of how long I have been advocating for businesses to improve with technology, and how old I am.

My career in software projects began as a Super User on an SAP ERP rollout in the 1990s, which was a wonderful career taking me on SAP projects around the world. Super Users are commonly used in SAP projects; a 2018 survey found that 72% of the SAP community uses some form of the Super User Model[13] and Gartner Research have asserted that 'Super Users serve a critical role in providing high quality ERP support'.[14]

However, as my expertise grew in software training and change management on large transformational projects, I used Super User networks when implementing other systems and technology into global organisations. I am currently training in the intelligent automation space, and having Super Users and advocates is crucial to the success of the technology adoption and operating model.

Super Users will be suitable for software applications that are used by more than one team or business function, or for a large end user population. In short, whenever you are driving digital transformation in an organisation by introducing new technology, Super Users are a valuable asset. The list below is not exhaustive, but shows where I have seen Super Users used effectively:

- business intelligence dashboards and reporting software;
- content management systems;
- customer relationship management systems;
- Google Workspace (G Suite);
- ERP systems such as Infor and Oracle (see below for SAP);
- fintech systems;
- healthcare and patient record systems;

---

13 Luttrel, G. (2013) *Sustainable super user programs are built on a solid super user model.* SUNSource. https://blog. sapinsight.com/2014/03/10/sustainable-super-user-programs-are-built-on-a-solid-super-user-model/

14 Phelan, P. (2006) *Super user role is key to post-implementation support of ERP systems.* Gartner Research, ID: G00138658. https://www.slideshare.net/harbounp/superuserroleiskeytopostimplementation

- human resource management systems;
- laboratory information management systems;
- Microsoft Office Suite and Microsoft Power Apps;
- product information management or lifecycle systems;
- project management and collaboration software;
- quality management systems;
- robotic process automation (RPA) and intelligent automation software;
- Salesforce;
- SAP
  - ERP;
  - Hybris;
  - Ariba;
  - Concur;
  - APO;
  - S/4 Hana;
  - Cloud for Customer;
  - Success Factors;
  - Business One.
- supplier relationship management system;
- ticketing systems.

25 HOW CAN SUPER USERS IMPROVE SYSTEM ADOPTION?

Reinforcing the concept that the objective and purpose of Super User networks is to drive adoption of technology solutions for the long term, not just provide product training.

You've invested a lot of time and money in your system, and we've shown people how to use it – but, as we discussed in Chapter 15 on evaluation, we need them to adopt this new technology fully, to use it as often and effectively as we envisioned, and for the system to deliver on the objectives we implemented it for. This does not happen by accident; we don't just train them and move on to the next project. This is why we keep Super Users involved and why we take a continuous approach to advance users along the technology adoption curve (Figure 25.1).

Figure 25.1 Technology adoption curve (Source: Image adapted from Wikimedia Commons, Technology Adoption Lifecycle: https://commons.wikimedia.org/wiki/File:Technology-Adoption-Lifecycle. png, originally created by Geoffrey Moore (1991) *Crossing the Chasm.* Harper Business Press)

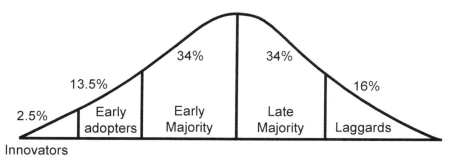

If we have implemented the ideas and concepts from this book, we have given ourselves the best chance of a successful system adoption.

We have:

1. Set the vision.

2. Used change management techniques.

3. Communicated it impactfully.

4. Built it correctly, simply and intuitively.

5. Trained it effectively.

6. Deployed it strategically.

7. Kept Super Users continually training and advocating the best practices.

8. Instilled an improvement and digital first mindset.

Here are some other tips on how Super Users can help with improving system adoption:

- Invite Super Users and business leaders to showcases or sprint reviews before product build is finished.
  - ○ I've seen many projects extended because a department head says, 'I wish it did x' at the end of a product build when the project plan was due to move onto training, but instead it had to go back into build.

- Involve end users in learning design in the case for change sessions, and involve Super Users by having them create their ideal session plans. When users feel it is their creation or ideas, they are more invested in seeing the project be successful.

- We use Super Users for training so the system knowledge and expertise sits within the business, with in-house experts, and not in the heads of a training or project team. Keep Super Users trained to an advanced level.

- Use Super Users to bridge the gap between technical and non-technical colleagues, by translating complex technical concepts into plain language for the end users who may be less familiar with the technology.

- Utilise ADKAR methodology and the technology adoption curve and encourage Super Users to give extra attention to the late adopters and laggards.

- Identify the early adopters and innovators and utilise them for communications and evangelising about the system. Earmark them for Super User roles when succession planning or in other career development opportunities.

- Continue your evaluation strategy and push to have the recommendations from your results implemented.

- Consider mascots, gimmicks or characters to embody your technology:
  - ○ Name your software robots; humanise your AI chat bot; brand a character to communicate the new features of your system.

- Consider gamification or rewards for correct usage or high levels of activity in the software.

- Develop a working relationship between your UX team and your Super Users. Aim to keep the system interface and configuration intuitive, and any prompts, errors or pop-up messages appearing on the system should be in simple, plain English, conversational and human.

- Communicate new features, fixes, upgrades and enhancements with maximum impact:
  - ○ Use Super Users for events, engaging communications, demonstrations, training and testimonials.

- Use data visualisation and business intelligence tools to demonstrate the operational impact of your new system.

- Communicate successes, wins and stories as a result of the new system usage.

- Establish clear metrics and goals for system usage and track progress towards those goals to encourage accountability and demonstrate the system's value.

- Insist on leadership and managers driving desired behaviours and leading by example:

  - Ensure your managers and leaders understand they are accountable for digital adoption, and that Super Users are there to support their efforts.

  - Have your CEO or project sponsor publicly thank a Super User for training them or solving an issue for them.

  - Make sure leaders show they are using the system themselves.

  - Offer one to one mentorship and training on system usage for your leaders. (Allow me to say that this group sometimes has self-imposed constraints on admitting they need training or advice in front of others. Reverse mentoring is also a great initiative for this.)

- Make sure Super Users remain in place for the life of the system, empowered to own training and instigate their own improvement ideas and system enhancements.

26 HOW CAN WE SUSTAIN OUR SUPER USER COMMUNITY?

How and why to maintain your Super User network coverage and keep the model in place for the life of the system.

If you are up to this part, then first revisit Chapter 7, and ensure you did everything recommended to create that Super User community. I could just say carry it on, and end this chapter here, but let us remind ourselves:

- Maintain coverage of Super Users with attrition and succession planning.

- Make sure your Super User network has an owner to keep driving community calls, maintain coverage and the cascading of future training and process improvements.

- Plan career development carefully for Super Users – we want them to progress and be promoted and be treated like the talent they are, and that is why we need replacements identified. But perhaps the positions are not there yet; it can be difficult to keep a Super User motivated after a big project. You can feel very deflated going back to the 'day job' so we need to continue responsibilities of process improvement, problem solving, development testing, onboarding new colleagues and ongoing training activities.

- Provide personal and professional development opportunities or other project secondments for Super Users.

- Encourage Super Users to share their knowledge and skills with colleagues and to seek out new training opportunities themselves.

- Offer opportunities for Super Users to network, collaborate and share best practices with their peers, both within the organisation and with other companies.

- Consider what skills gaps you have in your organisation: your Super Users have proven to be ideal people to retrain and upskill for the next step in your digital transformation journey.

- Keep your Super User community calls going at least once a quarter.

- Rotate Super Users to host community calls and to write any communications content. (Consider using a randomisation tool such as Spin The Wheel to select your next host to prevent it always being the same ones.)

- Hold your Super Users accountable for onboarding new colleagues and delivering ongoing training. It is not enough to attend the community calls; they need to commit to actions. Make sure Super Users actively ensure it is only them training new users, not other people, so only the official 'best practice' way is passed on.

- With some Super Users, unfortunately, you may have to check that end user training is still happening, as they may after time lose their enthusiasm and engagement. If you are seeing lack of engagement from your Super Users, discuss with your sponsor or change manager what you can do to address this. Giving Super Users specific objectives as part of their performance reviews is a good way to allow us and their managers to track this. Provide regular feedback to Super Users on their performance and contributions, including both positive feedback and areas for improvement.

- Keep a current list of Super Users, their departments, locations and areas of subject matter expertise. This will help to ensure coverage but also this list needs to be visible to the organisation, so they know who to contact.

- Consider pulse surveys with your Super Users: are they happy, motivated, supported?

- Consider establishing a formal mentorship programme to support Super Users in their ongoing development and career growth.

- Celebrate the successes of the Super User programme and its contributions to the organisation, both internally and externally.

- Continue to make use of them. Make sure the IT, testing, development and comms teams are keeping up that working relationship with them and informing them of activities.

- Keep up recognition activities: highlight Super User effort to the business continually. Invite leadership to Super User calls for that personal touch. Advocate for your Super Users and their ideas.

- After some time though, and especially after a huge, draining project, recognition only is not enough to retain your best people. Give them pay raises, give them bonuses, give them promotions, give them monetary rewards.

27 CONCLUSION

Concluding thoughts on why you should use a Super User Model for training and change management to drive digital transformation on software projects.

Investing in a Super User network of trained professionals can be a game-changer for businesses aiming to drive digital transformation and technology adoption. We have together discussed how effective project management, valuable communication and good leadership are undoubtedly crucial elements needed to bring about change; however, empowering a network of skilled professionals to promote excellence and enhance capability can deliver unmatched benefits.

My experience has shown that training Super Users and providing them with the resources they need to succeed can not only improve the overall level of expertise within an organisation but also increase the chances of successful project delivery. Super Users act as advocates for new technology and digital initiatives while also providing support and training to their colleagues. Their knowledge and enthusiasm can help to bridge the gap between technological advancements and employee adoption, which will lead to better business outcomes. I am a firm believer that investing in a well-trained and empowered Super User network should be an integral part of any company's digital transformation strategy.

Digital transformation has become a crucial aspect of modern businesses, and rapid software adoption is a fundamental part of it. With advances in technology coming fast, organisations need to find a way to react quickly to changes and to incorporate emerging technological advances to remain competitive. 'At least 40% of businesses will die in the next 10 years ... if they don't figure out how to change their entire company to accommodate new technologies.'[15]

I have spent 25 years in software implementation and have witnessed first-hand how utilising a Super User network leads to successful software adoption. Super Users possess a deep understanding of the software, are capable of leading training sessions, help teams adapt to change and are well-equipped to provide expert guidance when needed to both the project team and to the end users. When you give them the encouragement and permission to be proactive, they will become leaders in driving innovation and initiating process improvements, qualities that the workforces of the future need.

The main benefit of engaging Super Users is that they are already familiar with the existing infrastructure and processes that the new software needs to integrate with, and we need this insight to steer the right product solution. This can save you from having to

---

15 Chambers, J. (2015) *Why 40% of businesses will die in the next 10 years.* Ross & Ross International. https://www.rossross.com/blog/40-percent-of-businesses-today-will-die-in-10-years

invest in expensive external consultants. By tapping into this network of highly skilled individuals, organisations can ensure that their software is adopted successfully and that end users can seamlessly and quickly integrate new technology into their daily workflows.

If you want to achieve the success you need, you must remember that your people are always worth investing in. Super Users are an invaluable asset to any organisation looking to adopt new software. Without them, the process can be incredibly complex and time consuming. If you can afford to buy the new software, then you cannot afford **not** to use Super Users to drive change and promote excellence.

Key takeaways:

- Secure buy-in from your project sponsor to onboard Super Users at the design and build stage, and to keep them as a permanent responsibility after Go Live.

- Recruit the best of the best to be Super Users and treat them as talent to be developed.

- Develop a formal training plan for approval that adheres to the ADDIE training development model and commits Super Users to being responsible for future colleague training.

- Provide a blended learning programme that covers the categories of 'See It; Try It; Do It'.

- Establish a knowledge management repository for end users to access information.

- Work to your budget: a screen recording and PDF documents are adequate for software training, but aim towards immersive elearning, guided practice sessions and in-app training experiences.

- Insist on having a test or practice system, and allow end users to access it for independent practice outside formal training sessions.

- Incorporate a defect resolution stage into your project plan, to prevent a training window being squeezed by the inevitable retesting work required.

- Change management is key to gain buy-in, articulate the vision, understand the case for change, and to give end users the opportunity to discuss their response to the change.

- Enable end users to state their preference for training methods, and give Super Users the responsibility for finalising training session plans.

- Use Super Users both as system experts and change agents, and provide change education and train the trainer courses.

- Provide advanced system training sessions for Super Users, but there is no better training than testing the system.

- Ensure Super Users own and validate any data to be migrated to your new software.

- Give Super Users a voice and vote at any business readiness meetings.

- Be prepared to extend hypercare so it is ended only when all users are trained, incidents are within an acceptable level and process adoption is evidently progressing.

- Use KPIs for performance reviews to give accountability to Super Users to continue activities such as training, support and process improvement in BAU.

- Use Super Users as a key resource for process re-engineering to adapt your organisation to fit the future of work and new and emerging technology.

- Emphasise the importance of continuing Super User community calls.

- Use the Eleven Step Super User Change Model in Chapter 17 as your framework to evangelise, listen, educate, validate, execute and nurture and you shouldn't go wrong.

Some amazing change leaders' views on Super User networks

'Utilising innovators and early adopters as Super Users has repeatedly demonstrated significant benefits with both the sharing of system knowledge and equally importantly the change management required to successfully land digital transformation within an organisation.' Steve Motley, Digital Director

'Projects come and go but the software products they create have to sustain the business when the project is gone; the Super User is the critical role that binds this together; assuring fit-for-purpose design, smooth deployment & adoption, and maximising the value and life of the asset. Don't invest or deploy without them.' Chris Cook, Vice President IT & Global Operations

'To not involve those people impacted by change in the decisions, planning and delivery, is to leave the realisation of your desired benefits to serendipity.' Darren Ford, Head of Organisational Design & Learning & Development

'Super Users are a vital part of any project methodology, no matter what type of change you are driving in your organisation. Often delivery can be impacted and at times drawn out longer than necessary due to the lack of understanding or assumptions made about how the business operates. This is where the power of the Super User comes into play, no one understands how the business works better than the people driving the organisation. No matter what change or implementation your project/ program is driving, the Super User will empower you to deliver accurately, at pace, and enable you to drive adoption and mitigate fear of change.' Emma Kirby-Kidd, Global Head of Robotic Operating Model

'In the world where AI is more and more integrated into most aspects of life, human capacities and capabilities are more enhanced than ever. Building a technology of the future is no longer about the product but about the people it serves and bringing them together for a better tomorrow. Any smart software company should champion the concept of Super Users by welcoming them as advisers throughout the release and change process – create opportunities for continuous education, unleash their potential, and watch them create magic for customers.' Ana Howes, Vice President, Customer Training and Enablement

'I've been part of a number of digital transformations and Super Users can lead digital adoption by creating front-line success and helping spread the word across the organisation.' Kerry Mickiewicz, Head of Organisational Development

'You can have the best technology, software, tools and vision, but without educating, embedding, and empowering the team, the change is not likely to be successful.' Priya Deo, Director of Training Curriculum and Certification

'One of the much-overlooked benefits is that of the morale of the Super Users. Involving them in training gives them an opportunity to share their expertise and feel valued for their contributions to the organisation. Change management is not just a buzzword, it's the deciding factor between the success and failure of digital transformation initiatives. Without a focus on managing the impact of change on employees, processes and technology, organisations risk creating chaos rather than innovation.' Neil How, Founder and Executive Director

'Super Users are fundamental to the success of any large IT transformation initiative. They are at the core, the foundation. They act as subject matter experts, data analysts, they test the solution. Once it is built their job doesn't end – they act as trainers for the end user community and support the Go Live. Arguably one of the most important roles in a deployment. Without them, any programme will struggle.' Alex Farmer, Senior Digital Transformation Executive

'The concept of Super Users is very powerful and something I have used several times whilst deploying Digital Transformation projects. Engaging with users early in the project helps to understand and determine business requirements to shape the future state processes and technology. Maintaining and developing the knowledge and expertise of the Super Users through the project lifecycle allows the team to pilot and learn from deployment of software and process change, refining as appropriate. The Super Users really come into their own during live delivery and embedding of the change. They champion the change, support colleagues in the new ways of working and are the conduit back to the project team, capturing feedback to drive refinements and improvements. I would always seek to develop a bank of Super Users when undertaking a transformational project.' Neil Cavill, Head of Strategic Projects

'Local Super Users are the SMEs in their fields. With their knowledge and experience, only they can define and train the most suitable process that combines the new software with the business ways of working. Engagement and communication are key in successful transformational projects because people are hardwired to resist change. No one better than the Super Users to regularly talk and explain to their day to day colleagues how the new software will be beneficial to them!' Paula Sousa, Operations Programme Manager

ACRONYMS AND GLOSSARY OF TERMS

Acronym	Term	Description
	Accessibility	Designing content to be accessible for all learners regardless of visual, auditory or learning differences.
	Action mapping	Instructional design method to identify the most efficient way to make a learner competent in a task.
ADDIE	**ADDIE Learning Development Model**	Learning design development process: **analysis, design, development, implementation and evaluation**.
	Agile	Project management method favouring results and developer output over documentation, using short bursts of work. Research agile principles to learn more.
	Andragogy	Theory referring to teaching adult learners.
AI	**Artificial intelligence**	Artificial intelligence describes the capability of a computer to imitate intelligent human behaviour.
	As-Is and **To-Be**	The current and desired future state of a system or process.
	Assessment	Method to determine or prove the learner is competent to execute a task after training.
	Authoring tool	Software used to create digital learning content.
	Benefits realisation	Tracking, monitoring and validating that expected benefits of the system or training have been achieved.
	Blended learning	Mixing methods and modalities to ensure learners experience different ways of receiving the training.

(Continued)

Table (Continued)

Acronym	Term	Description
	Bloom's Taxonomy	Categorisation to assist in writing learning objectives, consisting of: Knowledge, Comprehension, Application, Analysis, Synthesis and Evaluation.
	Bottleneck	A build-up of work in a specific area or process preventing efficient progress and flow of work.
	Branching	eLearning designed to present different outcomes depending on learner choices.
	Breakout rooms	Splitting into smaller training groups, physically or virtually, to facilitate discussion or activities.
BAU	Business as usual	The point when the system is operational, the project has ended, and the responsibilities and ways of working are owned by the business.
	Business case	A formal document used to gain approval for budget, resource allocation and scope agreement for a software project.
	Business process	An agreed way of executing a task or function to deliver consistent outcomes. This should be documented with both the system process and the end-to-end process from request to deliverable, which may involve more than one system or department.
	Business readiness	Assessing whether certain milestones or tasks have been met to agreed criteria, to indicate the business is ready to accept the new system into operation.
CoE	Centre of excellence	A team of skilled experts who focus on best practices and standards for a software product or business function.
	Certification	Proof that a course has been passed or qualification achieved. Also known as accreditation if provided by an approved third party.
	Change agent	An advocate or ambassador for an organisational change, who takes on specific change management activities for the project.

(Continued)

Table (Continued)

Acronym	Term	Description
	Change control	A framework to assess, approve and implement change requests to a software product that is already in operation.
	Change curve	An organisational change model to represent typical personal responses to experiencing change.
	Change resistance	A factor that can determine the willingness to accept new systems or ways of working. The cause and reasons for resistance should be investigated to see if they can be addressed.
	Chat bot	A computer program that uses natural language processing to assist in conversations with humans.
	Citizen developer	Advanced end user of no-code or low-code software based in operational business functions, outside the core development or CoE team.
	Cognitive load	The capacity of the working memory to take on new information, to be considered during learning design.
	Communications plan or strategy	A strategy to engage and communicate to different audiences in the organisation about the software, project and change.
	Communities of practice	A group of people with a common interest and goal to instil best practice standards.
	Competency	Ability to perform a task at the required skill level.
	Compliance	Demonstrating conformance to rules or regulations.
CSV	Computer systems validation	Documented evidence that the system performs consistently as designed and intended.
	Configuration	Typically refers to the layout, functions and options set for a system interface or process.
	Content mapping	Matching key messaging, existing material or required content to the deliverables or objectives of a training course.

(Continued)

Table (Continued)

Acronym	Term	Description
CI	Continuous improvement	Establishing an ongoing cycle of improving existing processes, systems or culture.
CPD	Continuous professional development	Ongoing commitment to maintain knowledge or learn new ideas about your chosen expertise.
CAPA	Corrective and preventive action	Implementing and improving organisational activities to mitigate errors, risks and issues.
CPA	Critical path analysis	Technique to graphically represent remaining activities and estimated time to complete.
	Cross-functional	People from different business functions working together, like in Super User networks, to a common goal.
	C-suite	The most senior executives of a company, such as the chief executive officer (CEO).
	Cutover	Detailed plan of activities for the final transition from legacy software to new software.
	Digital adoption	Reaching the point where users are using the technology to its full potential for maximum value realisation.
DAP	Digital adoption platform	Software designed to integrate product tours, step-by-step walkthroughs or 'How-To' videos directly into the user interface of the website or software.
	Digital skills	Computer-based skills to advance utilisation of technology in the workplace, although there will be different development paths of digital skills for different roles.
	Digital transformation	Strategically integrating digital technologies and solutions to sustain, modernise, improve and optimise an organisation.
	Double and single loop learning	Single loop learning instigates corrective action, whereas double loop learning investigates the cause and requires preventive action.
	eLearning	Delivery of training through digital resources, typically an online self-led training course.

(Continued)

Table (Continued)

Acronym	Term	Description
ELEVEN	Eleven Step Super User Change Model	A framework detailing 11 steps for utilising Super User networks to deliver change and digital transformation.
	End user	The people who will eventually use the software as part of their operational role.
ERP	Enterprise resource planning	Software for organisations to manage core operational areas, functions and processes.
	Evaluation	Gathering and analysing information to determine whether learning, project and system objectives have been met.
xAPI	Experience application programming interface	Additional data, beyond SCORM, that captures learner experience and insights.
	Experiential learning	Providing practical or simulated experiences to enable users to learn by doing.
	Extrinsic motivation	Motivated by external rewards, recognition or achievements.
	Focus group	A group of people who can provide feedback or opinions as part of a facilitated discussion.
FAQs	Frequently asked questions	List of questions and answers designed to address most common scenarios.
	Future of work	Trends and concepts impacting how the workplace, the workforce and the ways of working are evolving.
	Gagné's Nine Events of Instruction	An instructional model to steer the flow of a training course.
	Gamification	Adding game playing elements as an engagement technique in learning design.
	Go, No-Go decision	Final decision-making meeting to ensure the project has met all of its deliverables and that the testing gives us the confidence to put the project live. The meeting can have three outputs:
		Go – a project can proceed to live operation.
		No-Go – a project cannot proceed for specified reasons.
		Go with caveats – a project can proceed if certain caveats are reconciled within a set period of time.

(Continued)

Table (Continued)

Acronym	Term	Description
	Hackathon	A collaborative event or competition in which developers, designers or other professionals work together simultaneously to create a solution to a problem.
	Happy sheet	Basic feedback form to survey training attendees.
	Heatmapping	A visual representation of activity over time for each business area used as part of an organisational change management strategy to identify and mitigate high levels of activity or change.
	Hypercare	A period of time after Go Live with continued support from the project team to stabilise and embed the system before handing over to operational areas as business as usual (BAU).
	Impact analysis	An activity and documentation to capture the impact of a change in system or process on each business function or department. The output is to determine how to best train, manage or communicate the change to achieve the most desired outcome.
	Incident management	A process for IT to respond to system issues raised by users.
	Instructional design	Creation of training materials designed to effectively enable the learner to achieve the learning objective.
ILT	Instructor-led training	Live training led by an instructor either virtually or face to face.
IA	Intelligent automation	Software that links robotic process automation with cognitive computing advances such as AI and machine learning.
	Intrinsic motivation	Training designed to enhance feelings of internal reward or satisfaction in the learner.
	Job or training aid	Training material designed to provide clear and simple instructions to be used when executing the desired task.
JIT	Just in time training	Ensuring training material is available to be consumed by the learner at the point of use, rather than having to be remembered in advance.

(Continued)

Table (Continued)

Acronym	Term	Description
KPI	Key performance indicator	A measurable value used to evaluate and measure the success of a team or individual in achieving specific objectives or targets.
	Key user	Advanced system user who acts as a trainer during the launch of new software.
	Kinaesthetic	Providing practical hands-on training sessions.
	Kirkpatrick	A model to evaluate training.
	Knowledge management	Strategy to ensure key information can be created, managed, stored and accessed when needed.
	Leadership	Ability to lead a group of people or project.
L&D	Learning and development	Organisational function to enable skills development, personal growth and role competency for the workforce.
LMS	Learning management system	Software for the provision of educational content.
LNA	Learning needs analysis	Documentation to capture who needs training and on what, skill gap analysis and desired outcome, to give an informed insight into how training can meet the need.
	Learning objective (or outcome)	Articulates what the learner should know or be able to do by the end of the course.
	Learning styles	A learning preference, specifically a preference for how to learn to use a new system.
	Legacy system	The previous, outdated or decommissioned system that is being replaced by the new software in your project.
	Lessons learned	An exercise to gather positive and constructive feedback from the experience to determine if anything needs to be done differently the next time.
	Master data	Key static data about your business, for example customer, product or supplier details.
	Medium	The component or vehicle chosen to convey the learning, for example a video or elearning.

(Continued)

Table (Continued)

Acronym	Term	Description
	Mentor	A person of influence who can guide or advise in a chosen field of expertise.
	Metacognition	Encouraging the learner to be thinking about thinking, prompting the learner to reflect on their learning needs, identify their own skill gaps and think about how to develop strategies to overcome these challenges.
	Metaverse	An immersive virtual world intended to facilitate human interaction.
	Micro-learning	Splitting a topic into shorter, easy to consume, bursts or chunks.
	Milestones	A significant stage of a project when requirements or deliverables need to be proven to have been met.
MVP	Minimum viable product	The most simple, basic version of your software that could be built and still released to users, allowing for learning and subsequent updates with additional features. Later agile development phases may result in a minimum marketable product and then subsequent releases would fulfil delivery of all features from the defined scope.
	Mission statement	Succinct aspirational statement describing what you will do to achieve the strategic goals of the project, software or organisation. See 'Vision statement' below.
	Modality	The chosen method of delivering the training, for example classroom, virtual, self-paced online learning.
MoSCoW	MoSCoW prioritisation method	Categories of priority and importance for project requirements. Each requirement is prioritised as a 'must have', a 'should have', a 'could have' or a 'won't have'.
	Navigation	Providing instructions to users for how to navigate the user system interface including menus, icons, screen layouts and features.
	Onboarding	Integrating new people into an organisation, group or, in our case, a community of Super Users with a view to welcoming, educating and familiarising them with the project vision.

(Continued)

Table (Continued)

Acronym	Term	Description
OCM	Organisational change management	A framework to influence successful change in an organisation.
	Organisational culture	The values, ways of working and approach to change, people or projects that characterise the typical behaviour of an organisation.
OD	Organisational design	Reviewing the structure and hierarchy of an organisation to determine if changes are required.
	Pilot	A trial period where the software is released for a small group of users, with the intention of learning from this stage, before agreeing a full release to all end users.
	Power user	An end user with additional system access or administrative responsibilities.
	Project management	Techniques and tools to enable a team to work towards delivering a specific objective, for example a new software or technology implementation.
	Project plan	Detailed documentation or visual of the activities and timescales required to reach milestones or completion of a project.
ADKAR	Prosci® ADKAR Model	A model to measure **awareness, desire, knowledge, ability** and **reinforcement** of teams or individuals undergoing organisational change.
RAG	Red, amber, green rating system	A traffic light colour coding system to indicate the status of the criteria. Red indicates a significant risk to completion, amber indicates the present issues or delays that require close monitoring, and green indicates everything is on track.
	Re-engineering	Technique to improve or redesign a process.
RTM	Requirements traceability matrix	A matrix to correlate the relationship between initial software user requirements, documentation, testing outcomes and potential confirmation of inclusion in training courses.
RACI	Responsibility and Accountability matrix	Capturing who is **responsible, accountable, consulted** or **informed** for a specific task.

(Continued)

Table (Continued)

Acronym	Term	Description
	Responsive design	Designing digital content to be suitable for and adaptable to different screen sizes.
	Retention	Ability to remember acquired knowledge and apply the skill at a later date.
RAS	**Reticular activating system**	Part of the brain that filters information for our attention.
ROI	**Return on investment**	A metric used to evaluate the financial benefits or savings achieved by a training intervention compared to its implementation costs.
	Reverse mentoring	A mentoring approach where a senior staff member is mentored by a more junior colleague to gain new perspectives or acquire digital skills.
	Risk management	The process of identifying, documenting and monitoring potential risks to a project or organisation and developing actions to mitigate their impact.
	Roadmap	A visual representation of strategic steps to achieve a goal.
	Role play	A simulation of expected real-life scenarios in an educational environment.
	Role profile	A document that outlines the skills, knowledge, experience and behaviours required for a Super User.
	Rollout	The introduction of a system or training in phases to the whole organisation.
	Scope creep	When a project has undocumented or unapproved requirements that could impact its success.
	Scrum	A framework for meetings of teams developing software or content using agile methodology, including stand-ups, retrospectives and sprints.
	Secondment	A temporary role change in an organisation, for example typically into a Super User or project role.

(Continued)

189

Table (Continued)

Acronym	Term	Description
	See It; Try It; Do It	A strategy for creating blended learning programmes for software training, to ensure learners receive a training method in each category.
	Self-led learning	A programme designed to allow the user to decide what they learn, and at what pace.
SLA	Service level agreement	Agreement to outline the expected actions or response time to certain issues or requests.
	Session plan	Detailed plan of content, timing, resources and activities required for delivering live training in a virtual or classroom setting.
SCORM	Sharable Content Object Reference Model	Software package of an elearning course to enable reporting and other settings in an LMS.
	Simulation	Providing a system environment to enable users to practise new skills or software processes. This could be a copy of a live environment for training use, a test system or a simulated system screen created with authoring tools.
	Social learning group	A group of people who have attended training together who will continue to regularly interact through facilitated or independent social interactions, with the intention of developing and maintaining system skills or best practice.
SDLC	Software development life cycle	A framework indicating expected activities through the life of a system from development to decommission.
	Stage-gate	A project management approach that involves breaking a project into stages or phases, with each stage evaluated and approved before the next stage begins.
	Stakeholder engagement	The process of identifying, analysing, communicating and planning action to influence stakeholders to obtain their endorsement or support.
SOP	Standard operating procedure	Written instructions to describe the standard way of executing the task step by step.
	Storyboard	A visual draft with placeholders used to plan and approve an elearning course before it is developed.

(Continued)

Table (Continued)

Acronym	Term	Description
SME	Subject matter expert	A person with a high level of knowledge or expertise about a system or business process.
	Succession planning	Strategy to plan potential replacements for critical roles in the organisation, in the event of a key employee leaving.
	Super User	How have you got this far in the book? Go back to Chapter 1.
	Talent development or retention	A strategy to keep your high-performing employees challenged, satisfied and motivated.
	Team charter	A written agreement defining the goals, values and ways of working of a team.
	Technology adoption curve	Framework to describe typical stages of adoption, use or acceptance of new technology.
	The Three E's of Competency	A model to determine the competency level required to assist in learning design and evolving user maturity.
	Transactional data	Dynamic, changing data that often describes a time-stamped event such a customer order, a purchase, shipping data, etc. See 'Master data', above, for the static data that remains the same, such as product codes or customer account numbers.
	Upskilling	Training designed to improve and build on existing skills.
	Use case	Description or requirement for how a person would use the software and the purpose of that activity.
UAT	User acceptance testing	Testing done by the business as a final acceptance that the system has been built to requirements, without issues or bugs present.
UX	User experience	Designing a system to consider how an end user will feel when using the product, with the aim of making the software easy to understand and intuitive to use.
UI	User interface	How the system will look for the parts of the software that the users will interact with.

(Continued)

Table (Continued)

Acronym	Term	Description
	User maturity	Mapping the capability and competency level of system users.
	User requirements	Technical or operational requirements to be factored into software design to deliver a product that meets its intended purpose.
VARK	**VARK model for learning modality preference**	Model displaying learning styles of preferred modality: **visual (V), aural (A), read/write (R) and kinaesthetic (K)**.
	Virtual training	Classes typically led by a trainer that can be attended online. Referred to also as webinars or virtual instructor-led training.
	Vision statement	Succinct aspirational statement describing the strategic direction for your organisation, and detailing the reasoning why the change, or the software, is necessary to achieve your business goals.
	Visual aids	Instructional material to convey information visually, such as infographics, signage or posters.
	Waterfall	Linear project management methodology favouring complete documentation and delivered requirements before moving sequentially through project phases.
WIIFM	**What's In It For Me?**	A concept that considers how content, activities or effort will benefit learners.
	Whole Brain Learning	A model of learning designed to deliver blended training in multiple modalities to meet how different parts of the brain learn and different preferences, to enhance comprehension and retention.
	Wiki	A database of knowledge articles developed collaboratively by all users.
	Workshop	A training session involving a mix of theory, practice and collaborative working.

REFERENCES

The books and websites listed below provided inspiration and critical thinking for the chapters in this book. Footnotes have been provided throughout the chapters for any works that have been quoted directly.

Sources for Chapter 1 'Why Do We Need Super Users?'

- Sinek, S. (2009) *How great leaders inspire action*, TED. https://www.ted.com/talks/simon_sinek_how_great_leaders_inspire_action

Sources for Chapter 2 'Is a Super User the Right Role for Your Software Project?'

- Pesoa, L.M. (2018) *The super user role: an extended concept.* BP Trends. https://www.bptrends.com/the-super-user-role-an-extended-concept/

Sources for Chapter 4 'What Will a Super User Do?...'

- Gupta, D. (2022) *The learning curve theory.* WhatFix. https://whatfix.com/blog/learning-curve/

- Brush, K. (2023) *MoSCoW method.* TechTarget. https://www.techtarget.com/searchsoftwarequality/definition/MoSCoW-method

- Hunt, R. (2014) *Super users.* BCS. https://www.bcs.org/articles-opinion-and-research/super-users/

Sources for Chapter 5 'How Do We Recruit and Select Our Super Users?'

- The HCI Group (2016) *Go-live support: training and super-user support.* HCI Group. https://blog.thehcigroup.com/go-live-support-training-and-super-user-support

- Faerber, C. (2016) *Stories from the field: 5 steps to building a super user network.* SAP. https://blogs.sap.com/2016/10/26/stories-field-5-steps-building-super-user-network/

- Kemah Bay Marketing (2012) *Analysis of the SAP Super User: Rebirth of a Popular Model.* Kemah Bay Marketing, Kindle edition.

- Obwegeser, N., Danielsen, P., Hansen, K.S., Helt, M.A. & Nielsen, L.H. (2019) Selection and training of super-users for ERP implementation projects. *Journal of Information Technology Case and Application Research,* 21 (2). 74–89. https://www.tandfonline.com/doi/abs/10.1080/15228053.2019.1631606

- Vaag, J.R., Sætren, G.B., Halvorsen, T.H., & Sørgård, S.D. (2022) A psychological investigation of selection criteria for learning agents (super users) and allocation of responsibilities in the implementation of technological change. *Frontiers in Psychology*, 13. https://doi.org/10.3389/fpsyg.2022.928217

Sources for Chapter 8 'How Do We Develop a Change Management Plan?'

- Healthskills (no date) *Accepting what is.* HealthSkills. https://healthskills.co.uk/article/accepting-what-is/

- Lopez, A. (2021) *Stakeholder mapping 101.* ProjectManager. https://www.projectmanager.com/blog/stakeholder-mapping-guide

- Prosci (no date) *Change management at the project level.* Prosci. https://www.prosci.com/resources/articles/change-management-at-the-project-level

- Nohria, N. & Beer, M. (2000) Cracking the code of change. *Harvard Business Review.* https://hbr.org/2000/05/cracking-the-code-of-change

- Smith, R., King, D., Sidhu, R. & Skelsey, D. (2015) *The Effective Change Manager's Handbook.* Kogan Page Ltd.

- Watson, R. (2021) *How to tackle any challenging change risks with change impact analysis.* Stracl. https://stracl.com/blog/how-to-tackle-change-risks-with-change-impact-analysis

Sources for Chapter 9 'How Do We Develop a Communication Plan?'

- CFI (2022) *The attention, interest, desire, and action model.* Corporate Finance Institute. https://corporatefinanceinstitute.com/resources/management/aida-model-marketing/

Sources for Chapter 10 'How Do We Develop a Training Plan?'

- Anderson, L. & Krathwohl, D. (2001) *A Taxonomy for Learning, Teaching, and Assessing: A Revision of Bloom's Taxonomy of Educational Objectives.* Longman.

- Branch, R. (2009) *Instructional Design: The ADDIE Approach.* Springer Publishing.

Sources for Chapter 13 'How Do We Design eLearning for Software Training?'

- ELM Learning (2023) *Immersive v. interactive learning—what's the difference?* ELM Learning. https://elmlearning.com/blog/immersive-v-interactive-learning/

- Duncan, C. (2020) *Passive vs active learning.* ElearningWorld. https://www.elearningworld.org/passive-vs-active-learning-getting-your-digital-learners-moving-interactive-and-involved/

- Moore, C. (no date) *Action mapping on one page.* Cathy Moore Blog. https://blog.cathy-moore.com/online-learning-conference-anti-handout/

- Vogler, C. (2007) *The Writer's Journey: Mythic Structure for Writers.* Michael Wiese Productions.

- Long, J. (2016) *The importance of practice and our reluctance to do it*. Harvard Business Press. https://www.harvardbusiness.org/the-importance-of-practice-and-our-reluctance-to-do-it/

- Farrell, L. (2021) *Training & development quotes to motivate your L&D team*. Cognota. https://cognota.com/blog/training-and-development-quotes-to-motivate-your-ld-team/

Sources for Chapter 14 'How Do We Deliver Software Training?'

- Kurt, S. (2020) *Gagné's 9 events of instruction*. Education Library. https://educationlibrary.org/gagnes-nine-events-of-instruction/

- Hietanen, J.O., Peltola, M.J. & Hietanen, J.K. (2020) Psychophysiological responses to eye contact in a live interaction and in video call. *Psychophysiology*, 57 (6). e13587. http://dx.doi.org/10.1111/psyp.13587

- Kalyuga, S. & Sweller, J. (2014) The redundancy principle in multimedia learning. In: Mayer, R. (ed.). *The Cambridge Handbook of Multimedia Learning*. Cambridge University Press. https://doi.org/10.1017/CBO9781139547369.013

- Kirschner, P.A., Ayres, P. & Chandler, P. (2011) Contemporary cognitive load theory research: the good, the bad and the ugly. *Computers in Human Behavior*, 27 (1). 99–105. https://doi.org/10.1016/j.chb.2010.06.025

- VARK Learn Ltd (no date) *VARK modalities*. VARK. https://vark-learn.com/introduction-to-vark/the-vark-modalities/

Sources for Chapter 15 'How do we Evaluate the Training Strategy and User Adoption?'

- Bloom, E. (2022) *Training program evaluation: how to achieve perfection*. iSpring Solutions. https://www.ispringsolutions.com/blog/how-to-evaluate-a-training-program

- Colman, H. (2022) *What is xAPI?* iSpring Solutions. https://www.ispringsolutions.com/blog/what-is-xapi

Sources for Chapter 16 'How Do We Deploy Super Users Throughout the Software Life Cycle?'

- Sukumari, P. (2014) *What you should know about software training*. eLearning Industry. https://elearningindustry.com/know-software-training

Sources for Chapter 17 'How Can Change Management Theory Support the Super User Model?'

- TopRight Leadership (2022) *20 transformational quotes on change management*. TopRight Partners. https://www.toprightpartners.com/insights/20-transformational-quotes-on-change-management/

- Bryan, L. (2008) Enduring ideas: the 7S framework. *McKinsey Quarterly*. https://www.mckinsey.com/capabilities/strategy-and-corporate-finance/our-insights/enduring-ideas-the-7-s-framework

- Mind Tools (no date) *Kotter's 8 step change model*. Mind Tools. https://www.mindtools.com/a8nu5v5/kotters-8-step-change-model

- Raza, M. (2019) *Lewin's 3 stage model of change explained*. BMC Business of IT Blog. https://www.bmc.com/blogs/lewin-three-stage-model-change/

- Smith, R., King, D., Sidhu, R. & Skelsey, D. (2015) *The Effective Change Manager's Handbook*. Kogan Page Ltd.

- Rittenhouse, J. (2014) *Change Management as a Project: Building a PMO*. Project Management Institute.

Sources for Chapter 18 'How Can Neuroscience Theory Support the Super User Model?'

- Rollins, A. (no date) *The link between dopamine and learning outcomes*. 360 Learning. https://360learning.com/blog/dopamine-and-learning/

- Cerdán, A.G. (no date) *Mirror neurons: the most powerful learning tool*. CogniFit. https://blog.cognifit.com/mirror-neurons/

- Johns Hopkins Medicine (no date) *Brain anatomy and how the brain works*. Johns Hopkins Medicine. https://www.hopkinsmedicine.org/health/conditions-and-diseases/anatomy-of-the-brain

- Malamed, C. (2021) *Metacognition and learning*. The eLearning Coach. https://theelearningcoach.com/learning/metacognition-and-learning/

- Sousa, D.A. (2011) *How the Brain Learns* (4th edn). Corwin Press.

- Howard-Jones, P. & McGurk, J. (2014) *Fresh thinking in learning & development: neuroscience and learning*. CIPD. https://www.cipd.co.uk/Images/fresh-thinking-in-learning-and-development_2014-part-1-neuroscience-learning_tcm18-15114.pdf

- Willis, J. (2014) *The neuroscience behind stress and learning*. Edutopia. https://www.edutopia.org/blog/neuroscience-behind-stress-and-learning-judy-willis

- Kirschner, P.A., Sweller, J. & Clark, R.E. (2006) *Why minimal guidance during instruction does not work: an analysis of the failure of constructivist, discovery, problem-based, experiential, and inquiry-based teaching*. ArcheMedX. https://www.archemedx.com/learning-resources/learning-science/kirschner-why-minimal-guidance-during-instruction-does-not-work/

- Farrant, K. & Uddin, L.Q. (2015) Asymmetric development of dorsal and ventral attention networks in the human brain. *Development Cognitive Neuroscience*, 12. 165–174. https://doi.org/10.1016/j.dcn.2015.02.001

- *Psychology Today* (no date) Episodic memory. *Psychology Today*. https://www.psychologytoday.com/us/basics/memory/episodic-memory

- Bernard, S. (2010) *Neuroplasticity: learning physically changes the brain*. Edutopia. https://www.edutopia.org/neuroscience-brain-based-learning-neuroplasticity

- Carpenter, S.K. (2020) *Distributed practice or spacing effect*. Oxford Research. https://doi.org/10.1093/acrefore/9780190264093.013.859

- Spencer, J.P. (2020) The development of working memory. *Current Directions in Psychological Science*, 29 (6). 545–553. https://doi.org/10.1177/0963721420959835

- Collins, S. (2015) *Neuroscience for Learning and Development: How to Apply Neuroscience and Psychology for Improved Learning and Training*. Kogan Page Ltd.

- The Human Memory (2022) *Short-term (working) memory*. The Human Memory. https://human-memory.net/short-term-working-memory/

- Grossman T. (2013) The role of medial prefrontal cortex in early social cognition. *Frontiers in Human Neuroscience*, 7. https://www.frontiersin.org/articles/10.3389/fnhum.2013.00340/full

- Van Schneider, T. (2017) *If you want it, you might get it. The reticular activating system explained*. Medium. https://medium.com/desk-of-van-schneider/if-you-want-it-you-might-get-it-the-reticular-activating-system-explained-761b6ac14e53

Sources for Chapter 19 'How Can Adult Learning Theory Support the Super User Model?'

- Pappas, C. (2013) *The adult learning theory - andragogy - of Malcolm Knowles*. eLearning Industry. https://elearningindustry.com/the-adult-learning-theory-andragogy-of-malcolm-knowles

- Mezirow, J. (2009) Transformative learning theory. In: Mezirow, J. and Taylor, E.W. (eds). *Transformative Learning in Practise: Insights from Community*. Jossey-Bass.

- Meij, S. (no date) *Adult learning theory: what it is and how to apply it*. GoSkills. https://www.goskills.com/Resources/Adult-learning-theory

Sources for Chapter 20 'How Can Knowledge Management Theory Support the Super User Model?'

- Roberts, J. (2015) *A Very Short, Fairly Interesting and Reasonably Cheap Book About Knowledge Management*. SAGE Publications Ltd.

- Lave, J. & Wenger, E. (1991) *Situated Learning: Legitimate Peripheral Participation*. Cambridge University Press.

Sources for Chapter 21 'How Can Project Failure Research Support the Super User Model?'

- Pearce, S. (2003) *Government IT projects*. The Parliamentary Office of Science and Technology. https://www.parliament.uk/globalassets/documents/post/pr200.pdf

- Kimberling, E. (2019) *The biggest ERP failures of all time*. Third-Stage Consulting. https://www.thirdstage-consulting.com/the-biggest-erp-failures-of-all-time/

- Lawton, G. (2021) *7 notable ERP implementation failures and why they failed*. TechTarget. https://www.techtarget.com/searcherp/feature/7-reasons-for-ERP-implementation-failure

- Fruhlinger, J., Sayer, P. & Wailgum, T. (2022) *12 famous ERP disasters, dustups and disappointments*. CIO.com. https://www.cio.com/article/278677/enterprise-resource-planning-10-famous-erp-disasters-dustups-and-disappointments.html

- Percy, S. (2019) *Why do change programs fail?* Forbes. https://www.forbes.com/sites/sallypercy/2019/03/13/why-do-change-programs-fail/?sh=62090d32e48b
- Snapp, S. (2020) *A list of SAP implementation failures*. Brightwork Research. https://www.brightworkresearch.com/list-of-sap-implementation-failures/

Sources for Chapter 22 'How Can Leadership Theory Support the Super User Model?'

- Bass, B.M. and Riggio, R.E. (2006) *Transformational Leadership* (2nd edn). Routledge.
- Burkus, D. (2010) *Servant leadership theory*. David Burkus. https://davidburkus.com/2010/04/servant-leadership-theory/
- Goodreads (no date) *Jack Welch quotes*. Goodreads. https://www.goodreads.com/quotes/476679-good-business-leaders-create-a-vision-articulate-the-vision-passionately
- Cherry, K. (2022) *The 8 major theories of leadership*. Verywell Mind. https://www.verywellmind.com/leadership-theories-2795323#toc-situational-theories
- Zalani, R. (2019) *8 major leadership theories: strengths, weaknesses and examples*. Turned Twenty. https://turnedtwenty.com/leadership-theories/?utm_content=cmp-true

Sources for Chapter 24 'What Systems Can I Use Super Users With?'

- Luttrel, G. (2013) *Sustainable super user programs are built on a solid super user model*. SUNSource. https://blog.sapinsight.com/2014/03/10/sustainable-super-user-programs-are-built-on-a-solid-super-user-model/
- Phelan, P. (2006) *Super user role is key to post-implementation support of ERP systems*. Gartner Research, ID: G00138658. https://www.slideshare.net/harbounp/superuserroleiskeytopostimplementation

Sources for Chapter 27 'Conclusion'

- Chambers, J. (2015) *Why 40% of businesses will die in the next 10 years*. Ross & Ross International. https://www.rossross.com/blog/40-percent-of-businesses-today-will-die-in-10-years
- Karuppan, C.M. (2000) Training super users in large health care facilities. *Journal of Information Technology Management*, XI. 21–27. http://jitm.ubalt.edu/XI/article2.pdf

FURTHER READING

To advance your knowledge in this area, I would recommend the following books:

- CEdMA Europe (2019) *Technical Training Management*. BCS.
- Collins, S. (2019) *Neuroscience for Learning and Development: How to Apply Neuroscience and Psychology for Improved Learning and Training*. Kogan Page.
- Harrin, E. (2013) *Shortcuts to Success: Project Management in the Real World* (2nd edn). BCS.
- How, N. (2018) *Run Fast: The Definitive Guide to Accelerating Technology Projects*. Rethink Press.
- Luttrell, G. & Doane, M. (2017) *The Super User (R)Evolution*. Enterprise Alliance Press.
- Moore, C. (2017) *Map It: The Hands-On Guide To Strategic Training Design*. Montesa Press.
- Roberts, J. (2015) *A Very Short, Fairly Interesting and Reasonably Cheap Book About Knowledge Management*. SAGE.
- Smith, R., King, D., Sidhu, R. & Skelsey, D. (2015) *The Effective Change Manager's Handbook*. Kogan Page.

INDEX

www.ingramcontent.com/pod-product-compliance
Lightning Source LLC
Chambersburg PA
CBHW041007050326
40690CB00031B/5295